FORGOTTEN RAILWAYS VOL 9

North West England

JOHN MARSHALL

DAVID ST JOHN THOMAS PUBLISHER

THE FORGOTTEN RAILWAY SERIES
Edited by J. Allan Patmore

Vol 1 *North East England* by K. Hoole
Vol 2 *East Midlands* by P. Howard Anderson
Vol 3 *Chilterns & Cotswolds* by R. Davies and M. D. Grant
Vol 4 *North and Mid Wales* by Rex Christiansen
Vol 5 *Scotland* by John Thomas
Vol 6 *South East England* by H. P. White
Vol 7 *East Anglia* by R. S. Joby
Vol 8 *South Wales* by J. H. R. Page
Vol 9 *North West England* by John Marshall
Vol 10 *West Midlands* by Rex Christiansen
Vol 11 *Severn Valley and Welsh Border* by Rex Christiansen

British Library Cataloguing in Publication Data

Marshall, John, *b. 1922(May)*
    Forgotten railways, North West England—
    (Forgotten railways).
    I. Railroads—England, Northern—Abandonment
    I. Title   II. Series
    385'.09427   HE3019.N6/
    ISBN 0 946537 71 2

First published 1981 by David & Charles (Publishers) Limited
New edition published 1992 by David St John Thomas Publisher
© John Marshall 1981, 1992

Typeset by XL Publishing Services, Nairn
and printed in Great Britain
by Redwood Press, Melksham, Wiltshire
for David St John Thomas Publisher
PO Box 4, Nairn, Scotland IV12 4HU

Contents

Introduction

Modern railway history began in north-west England with the opening of the Liverpool & Manchester Railway on 15 September 1830. Soon, three branches connected it to Bolton, Warrington, Wigan and Preston, and before a decade had passed passengers could travel from Liverpool and Manchester to Birmingham and London. The 1840s saw connections established to Edinburgh and Glasgow, Leeds, York, Newcastle and Hull, and by the late 1850s the busy Lancashire & Yorkshire system connected nearly all the industrial towns west of the Pennines. Gaps were later filled in by the London & North Western, the Manchester, Sheffield & Lincolnshire, the Midland, and various joint lines to form a network of a density such as could be found nowhere else except around London, West Yorkshire and South Wales.

Its density, however, was to prove its downfall. By 1874 four routes connected Manchester and Liverpool and it was possible to travel more or less directly between many other places by at least two competing routes. With the decline of basic industries this was bound the change. The great Lancashire coalfield became exhausted, or labour costs made what was left of it too expensive to work. The growth of road transport, particularly after the 1955 railway strike, took away passengers and freight, and in 1975 soaring fares and charges resulted in a further decline. In most schools there are now whole classes of teenage children of whom not one has travelled in a train, and many more in which less than five have done so. For them even the existing railways are forgotten. Since 1960 there have been extensive closures. One has only to

5

compare a sixth edition one-inch Ordnance Survey map with the last impression of the seventh edition to see the extent of the contraction of the rail system in north-west England.

The area covered in this book is one of extreme contrast; from the flat, windswept Cheshire plain and the broad Dee Estuary, through the agricultural lands of the Fylde and the Lancashire coastal plain, on through the mountains of Cumbria to the flat lands adjoining the south side of the Solway and to the western slopes of the Pennines; from the dense industrial conurbations surrounding Manchester and Liverpool, and the towns of east Lancashire separated from each other by expanses of bleak moorland, to the sparsely-populated areas of west Lancashire and Cumbria. Here, in the Lake District and the western Pennine fells, we have some of the finest scenery in England and, in northern Cumbria, a great number of abandoned railways.

For many of the closures the railways have only themselves to blame. The construction of 'competing' lines, or of lines intended 'to keep another company out of the area' was often opposed by the directors of the railways themselves, and it was known that many of the lines would make a loss from the start because the districts could not produce enough traffic. It was argued that the losses which the company would sustain from the entry of a competing company into its territory would be greater than those involved in the construction and operation of the railway. The losses that would be sustained by the competing company seemed to be of no concern.

Other lines were built by small companies and later sold as loss-making concerns to the main railway companies who had most likely been operating them from the start, and who thereby obtained them for less than it would have cost to build. Elsewhere dense traffic drifted away as people's travelling habits changed imperceptibly from one generation to the next, and as other means of transport became available.

Today the whole area is strewn with closed railways, many of which offer some interesting walks. Such possibilities are described in the Gazetteer section at the end of the book. It must be stressed that some sections of abandoned railways have been bought by neighbouring landowners and it is advisable to seek permission before climbing over fences in a determined effort to walk the whole route. There may even be a bull around, as the author discovered once with total loss of dignity.

Old bridges and uncovered drains can present hazards, too. The author has grim recollections of almost falling through the deck of the old Midland viaduct near Barnsley. While one would hardly recommend roping-up as if for a glacier expedition, it is as well to be prepared. If, in the course of your walk, you find an old milepost or gradient post, do not dig it up and take it home; it is there for the interest of us all.

Abandoned railways can be a paradise for naturalists. Cuttings expose strata which may favour certain plants not found in the surrounding district. Also, trains create draughts which carry seeds along, so that we can find strange plants growing miles away from where they are common. So, if you find strange plants, do not dig them up to plant in your garden where they will probably die; leave them for others to enjoy.

By all means let us explore our abandoned railways and enjoy them where we can, but we should do so with a sense of responsibility. Fortunately some enlightened local authorities have taken-over the old tracks and have converted them into 'trails' or linear parks, such as on the Hooton–West Kirby, Oldham–Greenfield and Stalybridge–Micklehurst–Diggle lines. This is something we should do all we can to encourage.

In some areas, however, railway formations are being obliterated by vast mechanised landscaping operations, so that all traces of the railway are vanishing to such an extent that they would not even show on aerial photographs. An example of this can be found at Pennington, near Leigh in Lancashire. Further landscaping is taking place all around Wigan. It is in such areas that the abandoned railways will be completely forgotten and where the books in this series will be of greatest value in recording, for a future generation, something of a superseded transport system and of a vanished way of life.

CHAPTER 1

In and around Manchester

Bolton–Leigh–Kenyon Junction

Bolton's great industrial growth in the late eighteenth and early nineteenth centuries demanded good communications with the surrounding district and with neighbouring towns. From about 1770 turnpike roads were built to Manchester, Bury, Preston, Chorley and Blackburn. By 1805 the Manchester, Bolton & Bury canal was completed and connected by tramways to several collieries. At Manchester it joined the Mersey & Irwell Navigation, providing access to the Bridgewater canal, opened from Worsley to Manchester during 1759–65 and from Worsley through to the Mersey at Runcorn in 1776. In 1799–1800 a branch of the Bridgewater canal was opened to Leigh where, in 1821, it was joined by the Leigh branch of the Leeds & Liverpool canal. At Leigh it was only seven miles (11km) from Bolton, but intervening high ground made a connecting canal impracticable. The poor communications between Bolton and Leigh, and promise of traffic from collieries between, led to the formation of the Bolton & Leigh Railway Company in 1824 to construct a railway from Bolton to the Leeds & Liverpool canal at Leigh. George Stephenson was appointed engineer, and an Act was obtained in 1825. The engineer in charge of construction was Robert Daglish *senior* (1777–1865) who had been responsible for building the first steam locomotives to work in Lancashire, at Orrell colliery near Wigan in 1812–13. They were rack engines of the Blenkinsop/Murray type. The resident engineer was Robert Stephenson the elder (1788–1837), brother of George.

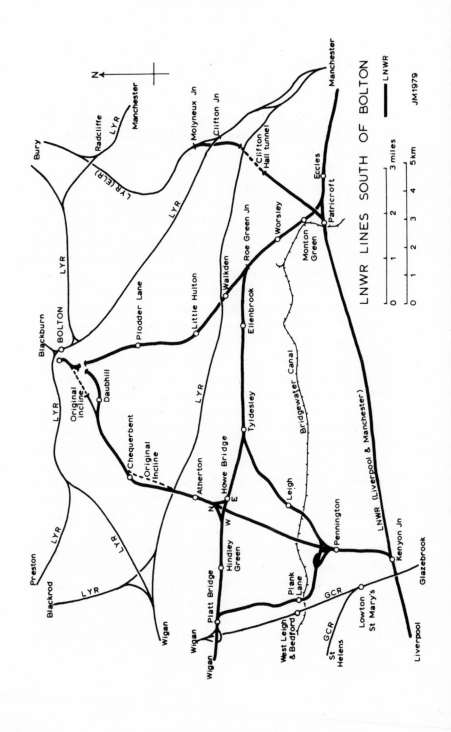

LNWR LINES SOUTH OF BOLTON

LNWR

JM1979

The Bolton & Leigh was designed like the Stockton & Darlington, Cromford & High Peak and other early railways, with stretches of easy grades connected by cable-worked inclines. With the inclines taking the place of locks, these railways were thus laid out in the manner of a canal and so formed a link between the ages of the canal and the railway. The single-track B&L railway, 7¾ miles (12.5km) long, was opened in August 1828 and so became the first public railway in Lancashire, though it carried freight only.

The line rose out of Bolton by the Daubhill incline, 62 chains (1.25km) long, on gradients of 1 in 33–55, worked on the main rope principle by a 20hp engine. A descent of about two miles (3.2km) at 1 in 425 brought the line to the summit of the Chequerbent incline 1 mile 20 chains (2km) at 1 in 30–49, worked on the same principle by a 50hp engine. Francis Whishaw, in his *Railways of Great Britain and Ireland* (1842), described the method of signalling for winding-up wagons: when all was ready at the bottom, the wagons were pulled back causing a spanner, placed on the rope at the top, to fall off.

The line was worked by some historic locomotives, the first being the 0–4–0 *Lancashire Witch* by Robert Stephenson & Co in 1828, which anticipated *Rocket* in the slanting position of its cylinders. It was the first locomotive whose cylinders drove directly onto the wheels through simple connecting rods. In 1830 the Union Foundry of Rothwell, Hick & Co, Bolton, produced its first locomotive, *Union*, for the B&L. This was a vertical-boiler machine with one pair of 5ft 0in (1.524m) driving wheels, and it had the distinction of being the first locomotive on which the cylinders were fixed to the frame instead of the boiler, unless one counts *Novelty* tried at Rainhill in 1829. It was the first of many locomotives built at Bolton.

To connect the Bolton & Leigh with the Liverpool & Manchester, then under construction, the Kenyon & Leigh Junction Railway was authorised in 1829 and was opened on 1 January 1831 for freight. Robert Stephenson, son of George, was engineer.

Two locomotives, to be named *Salamander* and *Veteran*, were ordered from John Crook & William Dean, Folds Road, Bolton, but the first of these did not arrive until May 1831. Meanwhile, overworking of *Union* led to a breakdown and while it was repaired Hackworth's *Sans Pareil* was borrowed from the Liverpool & Manchester where, after repair, it had been used following the Rainhill trials.

On 13 June 1831 a passenger service began between Bolton and Kenyon Junction, with stations at Daubhill, Chequerbent, Atherton, West Leigh and Pennington. At Bolton the station, on Great Moor Street, consisted of a shed terminated by a booking office, according to a contemporary account. At Kenyon Junction, where there was a 'lodge and waiting room', connection was made with trains to and from Liverpool and Manchester. Warrington became accessible from 25 July 1831, and with the completion of the North Union Railway, to Wigan in 1832 and Preston in 1838, Bolton passengers could travel via Kenyon Junction and Parkside to these places. On the opening of the Grand Junction Railway on 4 July 1837 and the London & Birmingham on 20 September 1838, Bolton passengers could reach London.

At Kenyon are remains of an east-north curve which, according to a contemporary account of the Liverpool & Manchester published in *The Penny Magazine* in 1833, was laid, though the 1847 six-inch OS map shows it as removed. It was included in the Act as a 'branch railway'.

A curious operating arrangement began in 1836 when the entire working of the line was handed-over to John Hargreaves *junior* (1800–74), son of a Bolton carrier. He ran the Bolton & Leigh with such success that he was soon in charge of the entire traffic, operating both locomotives and rolling stock. On 19 February 1841 he became carrier on the Bolton & Preston Railway of which he had become chairman in 1840, and he also took charge of the traffic on the Lancaster & Preston Junction Railway, opened on 26 June 1840. In 1845 he joined John Hick to establish the Bolton engineering firm of Hick Hargreaves, manufacturers of many early locomotives. He gave up his carrying trade on 31 December 1845, following

11

the absorption of the Bolton & Leigh, Leigh & Kenyon Junction and Liverpool & Manchester by the Grand Junction Railway Company. The following year this became part of the London & North Western Railway, together with the London & Birmingham and Manchester & Birmingham.

With the opening of the Manchester & Bolton Railway in 1838, the Bolton–Kenyon line lost most of its Manchester traffic, and for the next forty years the line carried on as a minor branch of the LNWR. Plans to improve Bolton station were discussed in 1855; it was demolished on 28 January 1858 when Trevithick 2–4–0 Side Tank Special No 156, *Redstart,* ran away with thirty-two wagons down Daubhill incline. Evidently rope operation had by then been abandoned.

By 1874, when the new Bolton station was opened (to be mentioned later), the single-line Bolton–Pennington section was a restriction, so a new double-track line on easier gradients, and with a covered way under a recreation ground at Bolton and new stations at Daubhill and Chequerbent, was built and opened in 1885. Even this new line dropped down from Chequerbent to Atherton at about 1 in 30; if this were not bad enough, mining subsidence at the lower end increased the slope until at one point it became 1 in 18½, one of the steepest gradients on a passenger line in Great Britain. The lower end of the Daubhill incline was retained to serve a short siding to a local brewery; into this were shunted tank wagons of water from Burton on Trent.

The Bolton–Kenyon line proved useful for connections from Bolton to Chester and North Wales, but passengers for Liverpool did better on the Lancashire & Yorkshire. Trains frequently stalled on Chequerbent bank, even with a banking engine, and had to set back to Atherton for another run at it. Another spectacular runaway occurred on Daubhill incline late on 16 March 1918 when a coal train, behind an 0–6–0 Special saddle tank, crashed through the goods yard wall and ended in the cellar of a house across Crook Street. Amazingly no-one was killed, but it took weeks to clear up the mess.

Beyond Crook Street yard a line ran through streets to serve the works of the Bolton Iron & Steel Co, the site of which is now Moor Lane bus station. This was formerly the engineering works of Rothwell & Co who, in 1854, built the extraordinary 7ft 0in (2134mm) gauge tank engines with 9ft 0in (2743mm) driving wheels for the Bristol & Exeter Railway. In 1906 the steelworks were taken-over by Henry Bessemer & Co Ltd. Beyond here, the line continued to the LNWR warehouse on Deansgate, near the junction with Moor Lane. Between 0800 and 0830 hours, traffic would be stopped on Crook Street and Great Moor Street while wagons were shunted across the road. On Great Moor Street the busy tram service would be obstructed, often for five minutes. The steelworks closed in 1926, and Deansgate warehouse in 1930. Nothing now remains to indicate that there ever was a railway here.

LNWR Eccles–Tyldesley–Wigan and Leigh

In the 1860s the LNWR was actively competing with the LYR for traffic in the Lancashire coalfield and between the major centres of the textile industry; both companies desired a shorter route between Manchester and Wigan. The LNWR route, via the Liverpool & Manchester to Parkside, and the LYR via Bolton were both circuitous. A plan for a line from Clifton, on the Manchester–Bolton line, to Wigan was included in a bill for the 1861 Session, but it was rejected in favour of the LNWR Eccles–Tyldesley & Wigan project, authorised in 1861.

The contract for this was awarded to Tredwell in August 1861, and in 1864 the railway was opened from the Liverpool & Manchester at Eccles to Wigan, with a branch from Tyldesley through Leigh to join the Bolton–Kenyon line at Pennington. From here to Kenyon Junction the old line was doubled. Where the Wigan line crossed over the Bolton & Leigh an east-north connection was put in and a passenger service was run between Manchester and Bolton via Tyldesley which lasted until 1942 despite its indirect distance of 18¼ miles (29.4km) compared with 10¾ miles (17.3km) by the LYR route. Besides these and the Manchester–Wigan trains, Tyldesley was also served by trains between Manchester and Liverpool via Leigh. Stations were originally at Worsley and Ellenbrook to the east of Tyldesley, and at Chowbent (later Howe Bridge), Hindley Green and Platt Bridge to the west. Monton Green, between Eccles and Worsley, opened later. A west-north curve on to the Bolton & Leigh, opened in 1883, was used by freight only.

The Tyldesley route was used by expresses between Manchester and Glasgow and Edinburgh, trains running non-stop between Manchester and Wigan, 18 miles (29km) in 30min. The LNWR 'residential' express between Manchester and Windermere also used this route.

With the opening of the Wigan Junction Railway (see page 94) in 1879, a connection was built from the Tyldesley line at Bickershaw West Junction to the WJR at Strangeways East Junction. At Strangeways West Junction, just beyond Hindley & Platt Bridge station, two connections, opened in 1880, joined the Lancashire Union Railways (see page 85). With the connection from Whelley Junction to Standish Junction, opened in 1882, a new route was opened from Manchester to Preston avoiding Wigan. The map on page 91 will make all this clear. Many through expresses used this route from the summer of 1887. Other services using this route were the Manchester–Windermere residentials and LNWR trains between Blackpool and Manchester, Leeds, Stockport and Leicester, and between Manchester and Keswick. The route continued in regular use for summer passenger workings until 3 September 1965, and from 6 July to 7 September 1968.

Local trains were well used and the Tyldesley line provided a good commuter service to Manchester, but it was easy to make it show a loss and, in the era of Beeching closures, the trains were withdrawn. Passenger trains between Tyldesley and Wigan, which were the least used, ended in 1968 and from Eccles through Leigh to Kenyon Junction in 1969.

Pennington–Platt Bridge

In 1885, in its urge to tap as much of the Lancashire coalfield as possible, the LNWR opened a 3½ mile (5.6km) double-track line, leaving the Kenyon–Bolton line at Pennington and joining the Tyldesley–Wigan line at Platt Bridge, connecting with collieries at Plank Lane and Bickershaw. By means of the Pennington avoiding line, or flyover, opened in 1903, a link from the Leigh–Pennington, over the Bolton line to a flying junction with the Platt Bridge line, a service of passenger trains was inaugurated between Leigh and Wigan. In 1910 there were three trains each way, one of them being the 1125 from Blackpool to Manchester which took this curious route. A station at Plank Lane, closed in 1915, served the colliery. Today all that is left is a single track from Wigan to Bickershaw colliery.

Roe Green Junction–Bolton

With the opening of the Eccles–Tyldesley line in 1864, the LNWR placed itself in a strategic position from which to construct a direct line to Bolton, striking off from Roe Green near Worsley. (See Plate 1.) Probably to avoid its appearing as a duplication of the established LYR route, it was projected in two parts: under an Act of 1865 from Roe Green Junction to Little Hulton to serve collieries, opened in 1870; and under an Act of 1869 for the 'Little Hulton Branch Extension' to Bolton. This included a new elevated station fronting on to Great Moor Street at Bolton, and another covered way 228yd (208m) long, under the Heywood recreation ground.

The new Great Moor Street station, opened in 1874, was used at first only by Leigh trains. It had four platforms covered by an overall roof, and a frontage described as 'in the Italian style'. (See Plate 2.) The 'extension' line was completed in 1874, and on 1 April 1875 a passenger service began, covering the 12 miles (19.3km) between Bolton and Manchester

Victoria. Its greatest asset was a service of through coaches via the South Junction line to Manchester London Road and London. With the opening of the Windsor Link between the LYR Bolton line and the South Junction line, on 16 May 1988, Bolton passengers again have a direct service across Manchester, sparing them the trek between Victoria and Piccadilly.

In 1875 a new engine shed was opened at Plodder Lane, about a mile out of Bolton. Here were stationed for many years the 0–6–2 'coal tanks' which worked most of the passenger trains on the two lines into Bolton, and the 0–8–0s which handled the heavy coal traffic. Lighter freight was handled by Webb 0–6–0s and in post-grouping days by Midland Class 4F 0–6–0s. Much of the freight work on these LNWR lines was worked by locomotives from Patricroft shed. A coveted duty for Plodder Lane men, who were largely restricted to local work, was to have a Patricroft Precursor 4–4–0 on a Chester job during the summer. In LMS days the LYR 2–4–2 tanks used to find their way into Great Moor Street station from Manchester. Later, the Ivatt and standard Class 2 2–6–2 tanks were used, and it was the latter which were operating the last passenger trains in 1954.

Passenger services on the former LNWR lines south of Bolton remained intact until 1942 when the lightly used Tyldesley–Bolton and Leigh–Wigan trains were withdrawn as a wartime economy measure. Passengers at Bolton, Walkden and Atherton were better served by trains on the former LYR routes, while traffic was also lost to electric trams and, later, buses. So, in 1954 all regular passenger services into Bolton Great Moor Street ended. Until 1959 Great Moor Street station was used in the summer for occasional excursions to resorts on the North Wales coast. Crook Street bridge at Bolton was removed in December 1966 and Great Moor Street station superstructure was demolished at about the same time. The elevated track bed was used as a car park until 1974, when the entire site was levelled.

Liverpool Road Station, Manchester

When the Liverpool & Manchester Railway was being planned there were several suggestions for terminal sites in Manchester. In the Act of 1826 the terminus was to be on the south side of the New Bailey prison. Before work began in Manchester another Act in 1829 authorised a new terminus beside Liverpool Road, a site giving convenient access to canal depots. The railway crossed the Irwell by a stone bridge of two arches, 63ft (19.2m) span, 53ft (16m) wide with 30ft (9m) clearance above the water, crossed Water Street by an iron bridge supported by rows of columns, and entered the terminus where there was a single passenger platform, a booking office approached by a flight of stairs from the front door, and a waiting room. Alongside was a large warehouse, and it was inside this, at the opening ceremony on 15 September 1830, that the Duke of Wellington and other dignitaries were entertained at a banquet. (See Plate 3.)

The occasion was inauspicious. It had been saddened by the accident to William Huskisson, Member of Parliament for Liverpool, at Parkside earlier in the day when he was run over by *Rocket*. He was taken to Eccles where he died later that day. There were angry mobs of demonstrators whose threatening behaviour caused the Manchester police to urge the Duke of Wellington to leave as early as possible because they could not guarantee his safety. As if to add to the misery of the occasion, the weather turned foul and the party was thoroughly soaked.

Liverpool Road station remained in use for passengers for nearly fourteen years. With the opening of the Manchester & Leeds Railway between Manchester and Normanton in 1841, connection was made via the York & North Midland with the Leeds & Selby (opened 23 September 1834) and the Hull & Selby (opened 1 July 1840), so providing a through rail connection between Manchester and Hull. Only the gap between the M&L terminus on Oldham Road and the L&M terminus on Liverpool Road in Manchester prevented through traffic between Liverpool and Hull. Several proposals were made for linking the two systems and, after protracted arguments, agreement was at length reached to build a central station at Hunts Bank, later named Victoria, with a connecting line from the M&L at Miles Platting and one from the L&M at Ordsall Lane.

Victoria station and the M&L link from Miles Platting were opened on 1 January 1844, followed by the link from Ordsall Lane on 4 May 1844. From that date Liverpool Road station was closed to passengers and became only a goods station.

The large 'new' warehouse was erected by Robert Neill & Son in 1880. The depot continued to handle most of the west side freight in Manchester until the rejection of wagon-load traffic by British Rail, after which it declined. Latterly it handled only sand. On 8 September 1975 the entire station was closed.

Liverpool Road station is an unpretentious building whose only claim to fame is that it is the oldest passenger station in the world to be served by locomotive-hauled trains. (Mount Clair station in Baltimore, Maryland, opened on 24 May 1830, and now forming part of the Baltimore & Ohio Railroad Museum, was used at first by horse-drawn trains.) Architecturally it is of little interest. Its plain two-storey frontage extends along Liverpool Road, and at rail level there is the original low platform with an awning, and the old booking office. The original bridge over Water Street, its jack-arched deck supported by rows of columns, was described as 'giving the appearance of the interior of a temple'. It was replaced by the present bridge in 1904. Beyond here is the stone arch bridge over the Irwell, difficult to see because it is sandwiched between the South Junction Railway bridge of 1849 on one side and by the ugly Prince's Road bridge on the other. With permission, access can be gained through a scrap dealer's yard from which a view may be obtained. It is not a pretty place, and the filthy river only adds to the gloom. To obtain the ultimate depressive effect it should be seen on a dull drizzly day in November or January.

Manchester Central Station and approaches

The railways of Manchester differ from those of Liverpool in that all the Manchester terminals were approached on viaducts; in fact most of the stations were built on viaducts. Manchester Central, itself on a viaduct, formed the terminus for the trains of the Cheshire lines to and from Liverpool Central, for Midland trains to and from London (St Pancras), and for various local services.

The passenger for Manchester from beneath Barlow's tremendous arched roof at St Pancras, after travelling via Derby, up the Derwent valley and through the great limestone gorges of the Wye to enter Manchester over the massive curving iron viaducts, alighted under Central station's arched roof, hardly less magnificent than that at St Pancras, and could be left with as fine an impression of his four-hour journey as today's 100mph traveller from Euston to Piccadilly in 2 hours 35 minutes. That is, of course, provided he did not turn to look back at the 'temporary' row of shabby wooden buildings as he left the station, but the monstrous pile of the Midland Hotel opposite probably took care of that.

The history of how the Midland reached Manchester can only be briefly sketched here. In 1863 it reached Buxton, but its route onward was blocked by the LNWR from Whaley Bridge. So it struck off from Blackwell Mill Junction lower down the Wye and built a line over Peak Forest and down through Doveholes tunnel to join the Manchester, Sheffield & Lincolnshire Railway branch from Hyde Junction to Hayfield at New Mills. This was opened to New Mills in 1865 and on 1 February 1867 Midland trains began running to Manchester London Road. Until the extension from Bedford to St Pancras opened on 1 October 1868 the Midland trains to London used the GNR into King's Cross. In 1869 the entire section from Hyde Junction to Hayfield was transferred to joint Midland/MS&L ownership. A more direct route from Romiley to Ashburys was opened jointly by the Midland and MS&L in 1875, on 17 May to goods and 2 August to passengers.

The history now becomes involved in the system of railways operated by the Cheshire Lines Committee. The main driving force behind this was Edward Watkin (1819–1901), general manager of the MS&L, who saw in a series of links a means whereby his traffic could reach the Mersey ports. He sought the co-operation of the GNR and LNWR, but the latter dropped out and in 1865, under the Cheshire Lines Transfer Act, the Stockport & Woodley Junction, the Stockport, Timperley & Altrincham, the Cheshire Midland, the West Cheshire, the Garston & Liverpool, and Liverpool Central station were vested in the GNR and MS&L with powers to the Midland to join as equal partner. A committee of management was appointed under the title of Cheshire Lines Committee, to which the Midland was appointed in 1866. It was not until 1875 that the Midland had direct access to the Cheshire Lines by a link from Romiley to the Stockport & Woodley Railway at Bredbury Junction, which it built jointly with the MS&L.

Under MS&L Acts of 1865–6 a new main line was built from a junction with the Manchester South Junction & Altrincham at Old Trafford, Manchester, to a junction at Cressington with the Garston & Liverpool Railway, and a branch from Glazebrook to Timperley, with powers for the GNR and the Midland to become joint owners, and for the lines to be vested in the CLC. This new line was opened to Manchester on 2 September 1873, and on 9 July 1877 was extended from Cornbrook over great iron lattice viaducts to a temporary station in Manchester behind the Free Trade Hall.

In connection with this, in 1873 the Manchester South District Railway was incorporated to construct a line from Manchester to Alderley which eventually became a link from Heaton Mersey Junction on the Stockport & Woodley to Throstle Nest Junction on the CLC extension to Manchester, opened on 1 January 1880. Until 1884 the MS&L operated a service from Manchester to Stockport over this line.

Meanwhile the CLC had almost completed its magnificent Central Station, shown in Plate 4. The substructure up to rail level was built by Robert Neill & Sons, who began it late in

1875. The enormous roof, 90ft (27.4m) above rail level, with a span of 210ft (64m), was built by Andrew Handyside & Co Ltd. It had seven platforms when opened on 1 July 1880; two more on the south side were added later.

It was intended to erect a large office block and hotel in the front of the station, and until this could be done a row of temporary wooden offices was built. But the Midland went ahead independently and built its own hotel, which still flourishes under private management. The 'temporary' buildings have been completely removed. On the site of the original temporary station a large goods station was built. On 2 August 1880 Midland trains abandoned London Road and began running via Stockport into Central using the joint connection from Romiley to Bredbury Junction.

To provide direct running to Central for MS&L trains, a further link round south Manchester from Chorlton Junction on the Manchester South District to the Sheffield main line at Fairfield was brought into use on 2 May 1892, and a connecting service was run from Guide Bridge to Central to link the Sheffield and Liverpool services. In 1899 the Great Central (successor to the MS&L from 1897) opened its new main line to London and began a competing service to Manchester, using the new route from Guide Bridge for through services to Liverpool. The section from Chorlton Junction to Throstle Nest Junction was transferred to the CLC on 1 October 1891.

Midland trains, however, still had to creep round the junctions at New Mills and Bredbury on a devious route. Spurred on by the opening of the GCR the Midland built a new cut-off from south of New Mills, through Disley tunnel, to Heaton Mersey Station Junction on the MSD, opened throughout on 4 May 1902 to goods and 1 July to passengers. At last Midland trains could run at express speeds almost into the heart of Manchester and could compete advantageously with the GCR.

Central became a busy station, with 400 trains arriving and departing daily. The trains presented a wide variety of locomotive types and carriages. CLC trains were worked mainly by

GCR (formerly MS&L) locomotives. The GNR, although one of the owning companies, came no nearer than Retford in Nottinghamshire and could reach the CLC only by running over the MS&L. Until both companies became part of the London & North Eastern Railway in 1923, GNR locomotives were rare visitors. After grouping, the Atlantics were fairly frequently seen. With its easy grades the CLC became the resort of the less powerful GCR locomotives, which lasted well beyond their normal time, the Pollitt 4–2–2s until 1927, and LNER D6 4–4–0s until 1947. After World War II one could still find trains worked by the ex-GCR D9 and Director 4–4–0s, but gradually these were displaced by LMS 2–6–4 tanks. At this period the CLC was handling the bulk of the Manchester–Liverpool traffic.

Local GCR services to Guide Bridge were worked by Pollitt 0–6–2 and 2–4–2 and Robinson 4–4–2 tanks, while the larger GCR locomotives were frequent visitors. From the Midland section, trains would come in behind Johnson 4–4–0s and 'singles' and later the Johnson and Deeley compound 4–4–0s, some of which worked through to Liverpool. Later the expresses from St Pancras were worked by Patriots, and the Stanier Jubilee and Class 5 4–6–0s.

In the early 1960s the main events of the day at Central were the 0745 departure and 2120 arrival of the diesel Midland Pullman multiple-unit train. With the coming of the Peak class diesel-electric locomotives, services were speeded up enormously, and at one period in the early 1960s early arrivals from St Pancras became an accepted phenomenon. By now the steam trains to Liverpool with their non-corridor compartment stock had been displaced by diesel multiple-unit trains, with little advantage in speed or comfort, but with economies in operating costs.

From 2 January 1967 the 'South District' locals were withdrawn. Chorlton-cum-Hardy, Didsbury, Cheadle Heath and Stockport Tiviot Dale stations were closed and the Chinley or Sheffield to Manchester 'all stations' trains from the Midland section were transferred to Piccadilly, as the former London

Road station was now called. Stockport Tiviot Dale station was demolished and most of the site has been obliterated by the M63 motorway.

During electrification of the former LNWR lines to Manchester the Midland route carried most of the Manchester – London traffic. But the vast expense of the electrification could be justified only by transferring all the traffic to the LNWR route. The Derby – Manchester Central stopping trains were withdrawn from 6 March 1967, with complete closure of the Romiley – Bredbury Junction link and Buxton Midland station and its connection to Millers Dale. Expresses from St Pancras and Derby continued to run into Central until 1 January 1968 when they were transferred to Piccadilly. These trains suffered a further setback on 1 July 1968 when they were re-routed via Chesterfield to allow closure of the Matlock – Peak Forest Junction section.

Lastly, from 5 May 1969, the CLC Liverpool trains were switched over a connection to the South Junction line to terminate at Oxford Road. Central station with its approach viaducts, and the South District Railway from Cheadle Heath and Heaton Mersey Junctions to Chorlton Junction, were abandoned entirely.

Manchester Central station has been converted into the Greater Manchester Exhibition and Event Centre (G–MEX), opened on 5 March 1986 and believed to be the largest unobstructed exhibition hall in Europe. There have been suggestions that the former Didsbury route might be re-opened as part of the new Light Rail Transit system, similar to the Bury – Altrincham 'Metrolink' line, work on which was in progress in 1991. The huge CLC warehouse was demolished in 1978, giving a view of Central from the north. Beyond the station further demolition work has opened views of the approach viaducts towering up beside the Bridgewater Canal basin.

Great Northern Railway Goods Station, Deansgate, Manchester

Another outcome of the MS&L London extension was a large goods station and warehouse erected beside Deansgate, Manchester, by the Great Northern Railway to enable it to compete for the Manchester freight traffic formerly handled by the MS&L from the GNR main line at Retford.

Parliamentary powers were obtained in 1895 and in 1896 work began on clearing the site. This involved the demolition of about nine acres of streets and houses including a brass foundry, numerous public houses, a school, a chapel and a burial ground. The site alone was valued at about £600,000 and the cost of erecting the goods station was about £1 million. The contract was let to Robert Neill & Sons of Manchester at the end of 1896, the work being carried out under Alexander Ross, chief engineer, and W. T. Foxlee, resident engineer. Work began early in 1897 and on 1 July 1898 the upper and lower yards were opened for traffic.

The warehouse was unique in being one of the first major steel-framed brick-panelled buildings in Britain. The entire work consumed 12,000 tons of steel, 25 million bricks, 50,000 tons of concrete and 1½ million granite sets and hardwood blocks. A typical 'aside' of the period, quoted in *The Engineer*, told us that if the rivets used in the steelwork were laid end to end they would extend for 65 miles (105km).

The railway yard was on two levels connected by two inclined ramps on gradients of 1 in 28. A short branch railway crossed Deansgate by a steel bridge of 112ft 4in (34.34m) span and led to a junction with the CLC Central Station branch. Beside the junction was a shunting neck and a small locomotive shed. There the GNR stationed the Ivatt 0–6–0 saddle tanks which would charge up the ramps with about eight wagons at a time. (See Plate 5.) Later, in LNER days, GER 0–6–0 tanks found employment there.

At street level wagons could be moved in and out of the warehouse either eight at a time by locomotives or, at the Peter

24

Street end, one at a time by hydraulic capstans and wagon turntables. On the upper level all shunting was done by loco-motives. Together the two levels could hold about 500 wagons. The five-storey warehouse measured 267ft (81.4m) long, 217ft (66.1m) wide and 75ft (22.9m) high. Besides rail access on the first floor an inclined roadway gave access from the corner of Watson Street and Peter Street. Along Watson Street were openings under which lorries could stand to be loaded or unloaded through hatches above by cranes on the first floor. The three floors above rail level were completed, with shops facing Deansgate, in 1900.

The Manchester & Salford Junction Canal, opened on 28 October 1839 to connect the Rochdale Canal with the River Irwell, passed through a tunnel 25ft (7.6m) below the GNR warehouse. Part of the canal, between Lower Mosley Street and Watson Street, was closed and filled in when Central Station was built, but the portion from there to the Irwell remained. By means of two hoist wells, access was made to the canal tunnel enabling traffic to be exchanged via the Irwell with the Manchester Ship Canal dock system. The M&S Junction Canal was last used in 1922 and was abandoned under the MSC Act of 1936 (No 124).

The GNR obtained access to the new goods station from Retford via Sheffield using running powers over the MS&L under an agreement made in 1892 and scheduled to the MS&L (Extension to London) Act of 1893. For many years a regular daily freight ran each way between Colwick, Nottingham and Manchester via the GNR Pinxton branch, a connection from this to the Midland Erewash Valley line, Pye Bridge, Ambergate, and then by the Midland route to Manchester. The warehouse and goods yard were used until 1954.

The warehouse is a vast structure, proclaiming in huge letters on all four sides **'GREAT NORTHERN RAILWAY COMPANY'S GOODS WAREHOUSE'**. Today it stands as a gaunt reminder of more prosperous days, while the spacious elevated yard forms a convenient car park for Manchester workers and shoppers and for patrons of the Hallé Orchestra in the neighbouring Free Trade Hall. Most of the low-level trackwork remains. The bridge over Deansgate was removed in 1970. The warehouse still stands as an example of one of the first steel-framed buildings, also as one of the earliest examples of a planned road/rail and canal interchange. It is used as a car park.

The Macclesfield, Bollington & Marple Railway

The railway first came to Macclesfield in 1845 when the Manchester & Birmingham completed its branch from Cheadle Hulme. With the opening of the North Staffordshire Railway from Stoke on Trent in 1849 Macclesfield was placed on a through route connecting Manchester with the Potteries.

By this time the Manchester & Birmingham had become a part of the LNWR, so Macclesfield became another frontier station between the NSR and the LNWR. As a means of reaching Manchester independently of the LNWR, the NSR formed an alliance with the MS&L for the construction of a railway from Macclesfield to Marple, where it would join the MS&L branch from Hyde. But by the time it was authorised in 1864 the NSR had reached agreements with the LNWR for through workings and thus the primary purpose of the line was lost.

However, construction went ahead, but painfully slowly, and it was not until 1869 that a single line of rails was ready and was opened for passenger trains. Even so, obstruction by the LNWR prevented the line entering the Hibel Road station at Macclesfield, and the joint line had to make do with a separate terminal station alongside the former Manchester & Birmingham terminus which had been closed to passengers since the opening of the NSR in 1849. Goods traffic began in 1870.

The following year an extension was completed to join the NSR six chains (120m) north of the NSR station (later

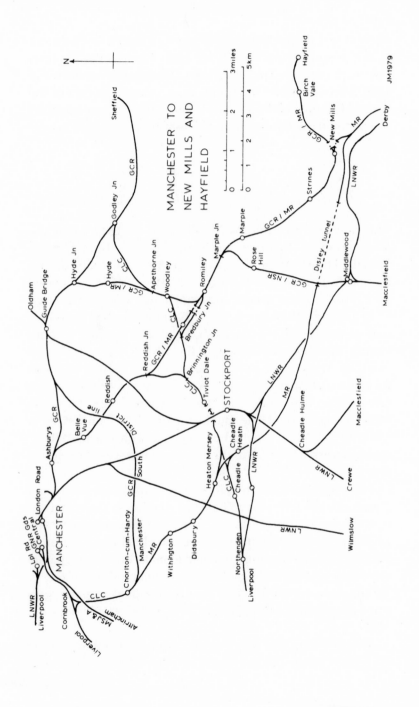

MANCHESTER TO
NEW MILLS AND
HAYFIELD

JM 1979

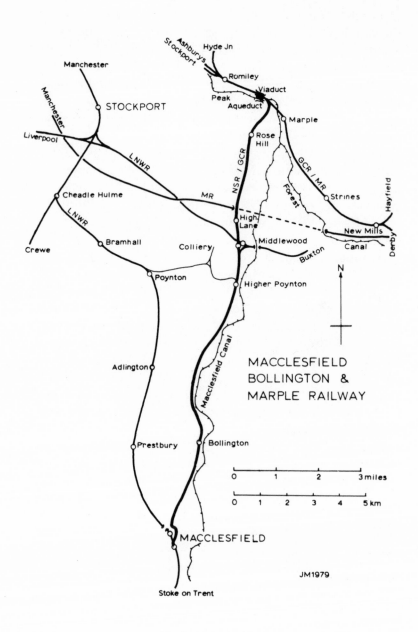

Manchester

STOCKPORT

Manchester

Liverpool

LNWR

Crewe

LNWR

Cheadle Hulme

Bramhall

MR

Poynton

Colliery

Adlington

Prestbury

Macclesfield Canal

Bollington

MACCLESFIELD

Stoke on Trent

Ashburys

Stockport

Hyde Jn

Romiley

Peak
Aqueduct

Viaduct

Marple

Rose
Hill

NSR / GCR

GCR / MR

Forest

Strines

Hayfield

High
Lane

Middlewood

Higher Poynton

Buxton

New Mills

Canal

Derby

N

MACCLESFIELD
BOLLINGTON &
MARPLE RAILWAY

0   1   2   3 miles

0   1   2   3   4   5 km

JM1979

Macclesfield Central) and was opened for goods trains. It left the joint line 13 chains (262m) short of its terminus and made a wide sweep round the LNWR goods station, formerly the Manchester & Birmingham terminus. At the same time the joint line was doubled and was opened as a double-track through route on 26 June 1871. Joint line passenger trains began using the NSR passenger station in 1873 and the former terminus was closed to passengers.

The only place of any significance on the line was Bollington, where there were a few mills. Just north of the station was the only major engineering work, a viaduct of 23 arches. A good deal of excavation was necessary, however, and in its 11 miles (18km) there were about 5 miles (8km) of cutting and a corresponding amount of embankment.

At Middlewood the line crossed over the Stockport, Disley & Whaley Bridge Railway, which had extended to Buxton in 1863 and had been absorbed by the LNWR in 1866. On 2 June 1879 a station was opened here on the Macclesfield line and shortly afterwards on the Buxton line. The opening of a connection between the two lines in 1885 enabled the NSR to run a Macclesfield–Buxton passenger service, though in summer only. This ended on 1 October 1914, but was re-instated from 1 May 1922 until 10 September 1927. The spur remained in use for goods and specials and excursions, the last of these running in 1954.

The joint line roughly paralleled the LNWR route to Manchester which provided a faster service with expresses covering the 17½ miles (28km) in about half-an-hour. On the joint line the 22¼ miles (36km) via Hyde took over 45 min. Macclesfield trains did not normally use the shorter route from Romiley to Manchester via Reddish, and nothing was gained by changing at Romiley.

Passenger trains were worked by MS&L, later GCR, locomotives from Gorton shed right into the 1950s. These were replaced by diesel multiple-units from 17 June 1957. The Sunday service was taken off after 16 September 1962, and goods traffic ended on 5 August 1968.

At Poynton (Higher Poynton from 13 April 1930) connection was made with Lord Vernon's collieries which supplied much of the mineral traffic until the collieries closed on 1 September 1935.

Latterly the busiest section was north of Marple Rose Hill which was used by commuters to Manchester. Since closure south of Marple in 1970 Rose Hill has remained the terminus of a well-used local service.

New Mills–Hayfield

The branch from the MS&L at Hyde Junction to New Mills and Hayfield was briefly mentioned on page 19 with the approaches to Manchester Central. In 1846 the Sheffield, Ashton & Manchester Railway obtained powers for a branch from Hyde to Whaley Bridge with a spur to Hayfield. The scheme had the support of the Manchester, Buxton, Matlock & Midlands Junction Railway company, which saw it as a means of gaining access to Manchester since its former route via Cheadle and the Manchester & Birmingham Railway had been blocked by the formation of the LNWR, of which the Manchester & Birmingham was a constituent.

On 28 October 1846 the contract for the Whaley Bridge and Hayfield branches was let to Miller & Blackie, but in the slump following the Railway Mania, shortage of money brought work to a halt in November 1847, by which time the SA&M had become the MS&L. In 1851, because no further work had been carried out since the end of 1848, and as traffic prospects were poor, the branch was abandoned beyond Hyde and the track was lifted.

It was revived again in 1856 with the intention of extending it to Buxton on the course of the Peak Forest Tramway which was owned by the MS&L, but by this time the Stockport, Disley & Whaley Bridge Railway, backed by the LNWR, was under construction. This was opened in 1857, so nothing came of the MS&L branch beyond an extension to Compstall, opened in

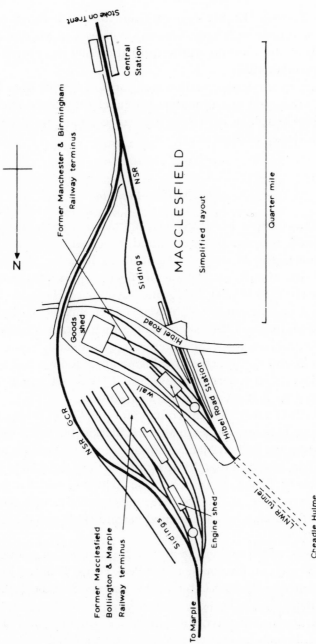

Stoke on Trent

Central Station

Former Manchester & Birmingham Railway terminus

NSR

Sidings

MACCLESFIELD

Simplified layout

Goods shed

Hibel Road

Hibel Road Station

wall

NSR / GCR

Engine shed

LNWR tunnel

Cheadle Hulme

Former Macclesfield Bollington & Marple Railway terminus

Sidings

To Marple

N

Quarter mile

1862. The remaining work was carried out by the Marple, New Mills & Hayfield Junction Railway Co, whose Act of incorporation in 1860 ruled that the MS&L might lease and work the line on completion. Meanwhile, the Midland, extending to Buxton from the Manchester, Buxton, Matlock & Midlands Junction at Rowsley, arranged to build an extension from its Buxton line at Blackwell Mill to join the Hayfield line at New Mills and in 1862 obtained an Act authorising this, a year before its line was completed into Buxton.

On 1 July 1865 the railway was opened from Compstall to New Mills, and on 1 February 1867 it was joined by the Midland from Blackwell Mill, so enabling the trains of the Midland Railway to reach Manchester London Road. The remaining 3 miles (4.8km) single-track extension from New Mills to Hayfield was opened to passenger trains on 1 March 1868. There was one intermediate station, at Birch Vale. The following year, on 24 December, the section from Hyde Junction to New Mills and Hayfield was transferred to joint MS&L/Midland ownership. The opening of the direct line from Romiley to Ashburys by the MS&L/Midland in 1875 shortened the route to Manchester by 2½ miles (4km), cutting 10–15 minutes off the journey time of stopping trains, and it was used by many of the Hayfield trains.

Hayfield is a small village at the edge of the Peak District, below Kinder Scout; an ideal starting point for rambles along the millstone edges, but hardly sufficient to provide profitable traffic for a branch railway. It formed the terminus of a local service from Manchester normally worked by MS&L, later GCR and LNER, tank locomotives and lastly by diesel multiple-units. It was busiest at summer weekends as parties of ramblers made for the hill tracks and returned in the evening.

The heaviest traffic on the branch was handled during construction of the Kinder reservoir above Hayfield, in 1903–12. A standard gauge railway was built from Hayfield to Booth Bridge about 1¼ miles up the valley, from where a 2ft 9in (838mm) gauge railway led up to the dam works. It was a 'wayleave' line, built by the contractor by arrangement with

Plates 1 and 2. Above: Class 8F 2–8–0 No 48276 and Class 5 4–6–0 No 45378 running light towards Eccles, past the site of Roe Green Junction, on 12 April 1962. The line to Bolton, by then disconnected, passed under the bridge behind the 2–8–0's tender. *Below*: Great Moore Street, Bolton, on 7 May 1966, shortly before demolition. The station was built by the LNWR in 1874. (*John Marshall*)

Plates 3 and 4. *Above*: Liverpool Road station, Manchester, passenger terminus of the Liverpool & Manchester Railway 1830–44. Photographed on 26 August 1975 shortly before closure to freight. The passenger station is on the right, with part of the shelter walled-up to form an enclosed space. The original goods warehouse, minus its awning over the tracks, is on the left. *Below*: Manchester Central station on 10 September 1967, with D117 (later 45 107) on the 16.50 to London St Pancras. (*John Marshall, T. A. Fletcher*)

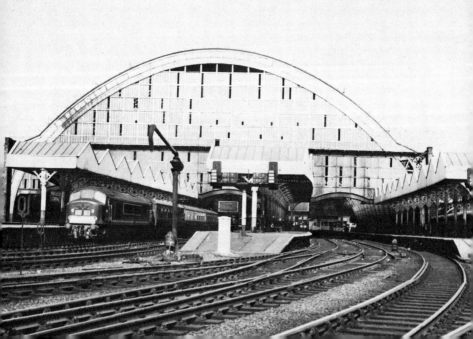

landowners. In 1906 the contractor failed and the works were taken-over by Stockport Corporation, which in 1908 obtained an Act for the standard gauge railway. At about the same time it was extended from Booth Bridge up to the dam site. Stockport Corporation ran a daily workmen's train of four-wheeled coaches, which became known as the 'Kinder Mail'. Traffic between the GCR/Midland goods yard and the reservoir railway was exchanged over a temporary connection across the road, in use for about an hour daily.

Following completion of the reservoir in 1912 the railway was dismantled in 1913 down to a site near Cuckoo's Nest quarry about ½ mile up the line, from where it was used until 1915 to bring stone from the quarry.

Freight traffic to Hayfield ended in 1963. Passenger services continued, with mounting losses. Opposition to their withdrawal came chiefly from ramblers who, however, did not provide sufficient traffic. Withdrawal of day return fare facilities only reduced the traffic further, until in 1970 the line was closed completely beyond New Mills. A remaining stub through the tunnel at New Mills is used as a siding for stabling stock for the Manchester local service. The remainder of the route has been landscaped, in places out of recognition, and a footpath follows its course to Hayfield. So today New Mills is the railhead for rambles on Kinder and the walker without a car has an additional three miles each way, albeit along a pleasant track.

CHAPTER 2

East Lancashire

The East Lancashire Railway

The East Lancashire Railway had the merit of passing through some of the most attractive scenery in Lancashire, and its abandoned routes provide the walker with some splendid tracks all within easy reach of the main centres of population. Further, they are scattered with fine viaducts and several tunnels to add interest to the journeys.

The main line, from Clifton Junction on the Manchester & Bolton Railway to Bury and Rawtenstall, was authorised in 1844 as the Manchester, Bury & Rossendale Railway. At the same time another company was formed under the title of the Blackburn, Burnley, Accrington & Colne Extension Railway, extending the main line of the MB&R to Accrington from Stubbins Junction just north of Ramsbottom. These lines became the East Lancashire Railway in 1845. The Clifton Junction–Bury–Rawtenstall section was opened in 1846, extended to Newchurch in 1848 and to Bacup in 1852.

The hilly country resulted in much excavation and heavy engineering; the River Irwell was crossed numerous times, beginning with a viaduct of thirteen arches at Clifton, and a fine bridge of five iron arch spans near Radcliffe. At Bury a magnificent block of buildings was erected to house the headquarters offices of the company. It was demolished in the late 1960s.

Beyond Bury the double-track line continued up the Irwell valley through Ramsbottom to Rawtenstall where it became single, passing through the narrow gorge above Waterfoot in two tunnels, Newchurch No 1, 162yd (148m), and No 2, 290yd (265m). When this section was doubled in 1878–81 there was

EAST LANCASHIRE

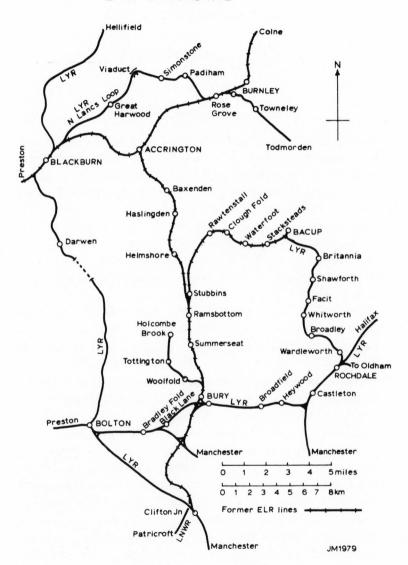

Hellifield

LYR

Viaduct · Simonstone · Padiham

LYR N Lancs Loop

Great Harwood

Rose Grove · BURNLEY · Colne · Towneley

Todmorden

Preston

BLACKBURN · ACCRINGTON

Baxenden

Haslingden · Rawtenstall · Clough Fold · Waterfoot · Stacksteads · BACUP

Darwen

Helmshore · LYR · Britannia

Shawforth

Facit

Stubbins

Ramsbottom · Whitworth

Holcombe Brook · Summerseat · Broadley

Wardleworth · Halifax

Tottington · LYR

Woolfold · To Oldham · ROCHDALE

Bradley Fold · Black Lane · BURY · LYR · Broadfield · Heywood · Castleton

Preston · BOLTON

LYR

Manchester · Manchester

Clifton Jn

Patricroft · LNWR

Manchester

N

0 1 2 3 4 5 miles
0 1 2 3 4 5 6 7 8 km

Former ELR lines ✦━✦━✦

JM1979

no room for an additional track in the gorge, so it had to be carried through the Thrutch tunnel, 592yd (541m), further into the hill (see Plate 7). At Bacup the old single-line tunnel, 114yd (104m), was enlarged. A new station was built at Bacup in 1880, in connection with the new line from Rochdale, dealt with later.

The extension lines were opened from Blackburn to Accrington and Stubbins Junction and to Burnley in 1848, and Burnley to Colne in 1849. From Stubbins, at a height of 442ft (135m), the extension line had to climb over a spur of the Pennines, through 5 miles (8km) of hilly country, to a summit at Baxenden at about 750ft (229m), with plenty of notable engineering features and some fine scenery on the way. The line crossed the Irwell twice, on the Alderbottom and Lumb viaducts, and there were two more viaducts at Ogden and Helmshore. Details of these are given in the Gazetteer on page 144. Beyond Haslingden tunnel and station the line reached the summit in a big cutting at Baxenden, from where it dropped steeply for 2 miles (3km) to reach Accrington at a height of 479ft (146m).

The notorious Baxenden Bank (see Plate 8), with its gradient of 1 in 40 was an operating problem from the start. The first sand drags on the LYR were installed on the bank in 1903 to retard any runaways. The most remarkable piece of operational skill resulted from the introduction of an Accrington slip coach off the 1625 express from Salford to Colne, in 1914. Despite use of train brakes in descending the bank, vacuum had to be restored before the coach was slipped to provide enough brake power for the slip portion, and because on the sharp curve through Accrington station the driver could not see if the slip had been successful, a man had to be stationed at a suitable place on the platform to signal to the driver that all was in order.

At Colne the ELR made an end-on junction with the Midland Railway whose line from Skipton, originally the Leeds & Bradford Railway, had opened on 2 October 1848, becoming absorbed in the Midland on 24 July 1851. It thus opened up a new route between Manchester and Bradford and Leeds, in opposition to the Lancashire & Yorkshire, which promptly began restrictive measures against the ELR at Clifton Junction from whence into Manchester the ELR exercised running powers over the LYR. This culminated in the 'Battle of Clifton Junction' on 12 March 1849 when the LYR forcibly stopped an ELR train, causing a complete blockage of its own traffic at the same time. (See *The Lancashire & Yorkshire Railway* Vol 1, pages 115–16.) An uneasy peace followed until, after several attempts at amalgamation had been strongly opposed by the Midland and the LNWR, the LYR/ELR Amalgamation Act was passed in 1859.

Another section of the ELR, the Blackburn & Preston Railway, was opened on 1 June 1846 to join the North Union Railway at Farington south of Preston. By means of the Liverpool, Ormskirk & Preston Railway, opened on 2 April 1849, the ELR gained access to Liverpool.

To reach Preston without using the NUR from Farington, the 'Preston Extension' was opened in 1850 from Bamber Bridge and Lostock Hall Junctions. It was built by McCormick & Daglish in 1848–50, and included a brick viaduct of 52 arches of 30ft (9.14m) span across the meadows south of the Ribble, leading to a bridge of three cast-iron arched spans over the river. The viaduct gave much trouble during floods, even though each pier stood on seventeen 12in (305mm) square beech piles. After some repairs in the 1860s it was decided in 1880 to convert it to an embankment, this being carried out in 1884–6. One arch remains as a bridge over a road, and two more at the approach to the Ribble bridge form flood openings. The coping stones along the top of the viaduct can still be seen along the embankment.

In 1883 the 'Preston Extension' was joined here, at what became Whitehouse South Junction, by the West Lancashire Railway extension, so making possible a through service between Southport and Blackburn (Chapter 4). Later, in 1900, the LYR opened the connection from the former WLR to Whitehouse South Junction, enabling it to close the Preston

WLR station. At Preston trains from the ELR line ran into a separate station alongside the joint LYR/LNWR main line station, beyond which the two lines joined. The cast-iron arches over the Ribble were replaced by steel girders in 1930.

Most services on the ELR section were short runs. The longest was Manchester–Colne, 34½ miles (55km). The Manchester–Bury–Accrington–Colne section handled a heavy commuter traffic, particularly on Tuesdays and Fridays when the directors of the cotton mills travelled to Manchester to make their cotton purchases at the Royal Exchange. For many years the heaviest passenger trains were handled by the Hughes superheated 2–4–2 Belpaire tanks, and later by his huge Baltic tanks, the 4–6–4T version of his four-cylinder 4–6–0. These in turn were displaced by the LMS 2–6–4 tanks, and during the 1960s by diesel multiple-units.

Freight traffic consisted of long coal trains to Goole or Liverpool and returning empties behind the LYR 0–8–0s, and vast quantities of coal, raw and processed cotton and finished products for the numerous mills everywhere, much of which would be handled by the LYR 0–6–0s. At the larger centres shunting went on day and night, generally with 0–6–0 tender or saddle tank locomotives. The entire system buzzed with activity.

The ELR remained complete, apart from the Skelmersdale branch, until 5 December 1966 when the sections from Clifton Junction to Radcliffe North Junction, Rawtenstall to Bacup, and Stubbins to Accrington were closed entirely. The Preston Extension was closed to passengers in 1968 and to goods in 1972. The last passenger trains between Bury and Rawtenstall ran on 3 June 1972 and the last coal train, via Heywood, consisting of eleven wagons and a brake van behind 40 098, ran on 4 December 1980.

Bury–Holcombe Brook

A branch from the former ELR main line, constructed independently, and operated by the LYR, was the single line from

Bury to Holcombe Brook, built by the Bury & Tottington District Railway Company and opened in 1882. Its shuttle service to and from Bury was enlivened in 1913 when Dick, Kerr & Co of Preston, which had provided equipment for the LYR Liverpool–Southport electrification, used the branch for an experiment in high-voltage dc electric traction, using an overhead line at 3600V. The experiment lasted until 1916 when Dick, Kerr handed the line back to the LYR, which then electrified it at 1200V dc using a side-contact third rail, as an extension of the Manchester–Bury system.

An electric shuttle service was operated between Bury and Holcombe Brook, generally with two-car sets, until the electrical equipment was ready for renewal. The expense of this was considered unjustifiable, so from 25 March 1951 a steam push-and-pull train was substituted, using an LYR 2–4–2 tank and railmotor coach until the passenger service was withdrawn on 5 May 1952. Freight ran to Holcombe Brook until 1960 when it was cut back to Tottington, and in 1963 the line was closed completely. No sooner had it closed than extensive housing development began all along its route. Today an electric train service might be useful, but parts of the line are built over.

Middleton Junction–Oldham Werneth

Oldham lies on rising ground seven miles (11km) north-east of Manchester and over 400ft (122m) higher. As a result of its position, transport to and from the town was difficult. The nearest canal was a branch of the Ashton Canal at Hollinwood Basin, almost 2 miles (3.2km) from the town centre and at a much lower level, as also was the Rochdale Canal.

As early as 1826 an Act (No 99) was obtained for the Manchester & Oldham Railway, but no work was carried out on the project. However, the Manchester & Leeds Railway, being projected at the same time, passed only two miles from Oldham, and in an Act of 1839 powers were obtained to construct a branch into the town. Meanwhile, a station was opened on the main line at Miils Hill for Oldham, on 4 July 1839.

The chief engineer of the Manchester & Leeds was George Stephenson, who still thought that steam locomotives would never be capable of climbing inclines much steeper than 1 in 100, so the branch was laid out with the climbing concentrated into ¾ mile at 1 in 27 on which trains would be assisted by a rope. This also avoided a long approach embankment which would have eased the gradient considerably. There were no heavy engineering works on the branch, which terminated at Werneth on the west side of Oldham. Work began on 29 July 1841 and the 1¾ mile (2.8km) line was opened in 1842. It climbed from 343ft (104.5m) above sea level at the junction to 525ft (160m) at Werneth station.

It was worked by a rope passing round a 17ft 0in (5.18m) diameter pulley at the top. One end was attached to the train and the other end to a balance load consisting of either wagons filled with sand, and a heavy brake van, or a load of coal from a colliery near the top. One track was used for the trains and the other for the balance load. Train loads were heavy; trains carrying 600 or 700 passengers ran frequently, while at times as many as 1,200 passengers were carried on one train. Speeds on the incline were from 20 to 25mph (32–40km/h). The wire rope, 1¼ miles long, weighed 6 tons 6cwt and lasted about two years, four months. Had the branch been built only ten years later, under Hawkshaw, it would most likely have been raised on an embankment at its lower end to ease the gradient.

On 1 November 1847 the branch was extended through two tunnels to Oldham Mumps, and in preparation for this Thomas Normington was appointed stationmaster of Mumps in October. Normington (1824–1916) ultimately became assitant superintendent at Wakefield, LYR, and after his retirement he wrote an entertaining book about his life on the LYR, published in 1898. His account of an experience on the Werneth line is worth quoting:

I well remember one day travelling by the last passenger

train from Manchester to Oldham. It consisted of five coaches and brake van, engine No 131, I think, which was a new one, the driver being William Bates. The engine being attached to the rope at the bottom of the incline in the usual way, the train travelled about half way up the incline, when the rope broke, and the train came to a stand. I went to the driver and asked him what he intended to do under the circumstances. He replied, 'It's all up, lad: we shall have to stop here all neet.' I said, 'Nonsense'; but he said the engine could not get up the incline itself without the rope. Seeing that it was a strong new engine, I suggested to the driver and the guard that we should set the train back to the bottom of the incline, and test the question. The train was set back, we got the passengers into two carriages, and shunted the other portion off into a siding. The engine was then coupled to the two coaches. The driver repeatedly declared that it was not possible to get up the incline, not even the engine alone, without the rope. However, I prevailed upon the driver to try, and after my explanation he agreed to try. The two coaches and brake van were then set back on the level some four hundred yards towards Middleton Junction. The driver gave a good start, and ran well up to within some three hundred yards of the top of the incline, when the train came to a stand. I told the driver he had not done his best, having no steam to start with. After some sharp words had passed between us, he agreed to make another trial. The train was again set back, a further distance on the level this time, and, steam being well up, we started again, and arrived safely at the top of the incline. The passengers gave a good hearty cheer for accomplishing what was considered to be an impossibility. This test resulted in more powerful engines being built, and the dispensing with ropes for assisting trains on all steep inclines. Mr William Hirst, then locomotive superintendent, [actually William Hurst, outdoor superintendent], accompanied by some of the directors, took charge of the first engine, No 151, which took the first passenger train of six coaches up the Oldham incline without the assistance of a rope, in June, 1851.

As this is written nearly fifty years after the event, its accuracy is dubious. 'Engine No 131' was a Jenkins 2–2–2 built by Bury, Curtis & Kennedy, Liverpool, in April 1849, which suggests that Normington's journey was in the summer of that year. No 151 was of the same class and make of August 1849. The Jenkins singles were pretty feeble, and most were later rebuilt into 2–4–0s. From about 1854 all trains mounted the bank by their own power, thanks to the possibility of a good run at the foot. On Sunday, 6 February 1859 the incline was used to test the Newall and Fay systems of continuous brakes.

On 17 May 1880 the direct line was opened from Thorpes Bridge Junction to Werneth, but passenger trains continued to use the original line from Middleton Junction until 1958. To the end they were steam-worked, for many years by the LYR 2–4–2 tanks and latterly by 2–6–4 tanks. It was an exciting experience to stand on Werneth station wondering if the ascending train would make it as it blasted its way up, past the junction of the Failsworth line, to crawl into the station at 10–15mph.

On Sundays during May 1960, while the Failsworth line was being re-ballasted, the old line was used again by passenger trains, this time by diesel multiple-units which were put to a severe test by the climb. Some in fact did not make it and had to set back for another try.

The last passenger train up the incline, in which the author was a passenger, was an enthusiasts' special on 17 September 1960. It consisted of four coaches headed by LYR 2–4–2 tank No 50850 and banked in the rear by LYR 0–6–0 No 52271. Occasional freight trains used the incline until 1963, when it was closed completely between the junction of the Chadderton branch and Werneth junciton, and it was dismantled in April 1964. Since then the course of the line has been obliterated under a general landscaping of the area.

Bolton–Bury–Castleton

The Liverpool & Manchester and its successors, the Grand Junction and LNWR, maintained a complete monopoly of rail traffic to Liverpool for eighteen years, during which time the population of Liverpool nearly doubled and the shipping trade at the port more than doubled. The monopoly was at last broken by the Liverpool & Bury Railway, connecting Liverpool with Wigan, Bolton and Bury and, by an LYR extension authorised in 1845, with the Manchester & Leeds main line south of Rochdale. In 1846 the L&B was amalgamated with the Manchester & Leeds, which became the LYR in 1847, and in 1848 the new lines were opened, on 1 May from Heywood to Bury and on 20 November from Liverpool to Lostock Junction, Bolton, and from Bolton to Bury. From Walton Junction to Liverpool, the route was owned jointly by the ELR and the LYR. At Lostock Junction it joined the former Bolton & Preston Railway, then owned by the North Union Railway Co. Beyond Bolton the Bury line left the Manchester line and crossed the Croal and Tonge valleys by high iron lattice deck-girder viaducts on stone piers, the first of their kind in England, as shown in Plate 6. Approaching Bury the line crossed the Manchester, Bolton & Bury canal and the Irwell by a stone viaduct. In connection with the Cheetham Hill, Manchester–Radcliffe line, opened in 1879, a link was opened from Radcliffe to join the Bolton–Bury line, so providing an alternative route between Bolton and Manchester.

All these lines carried heavy traffic, both passenger and freight, throughout the LYR and LMS periods. The Radcliffe–Bradley Fold link was used by the last of the LYR railmotors on a service to Bolton and Horwich until 1947. By the time of the Beeching cut-back traffic had declined considerably. From 5 October 1970, despite fierce local opposition, passenger trains between Bolton, Bury and Rochdale were withdrawn, and track was removed between Bolton and Bury. From Castleton to Bury and round the curve to the ELR and up to Rawtenstall a single line was retained for the occasional coal train. A new bus/rail interchange was opened at Bury on 17 March 1980 using part of the former Bury 'Loco Loop', opened in 1898 in connection with the Salford Dock branch, closed in 1967 and subsequently lifted. The opening of the new interchange brought about closure of the former ELR station at Bury Bolton Street. The single line to Rawtenstall crossed the new interchange tracks on the level at the site of the former Bury Knowsley Street station, but the crossing was short-lived because the last coal train ran on 4 December 1980. The line was closed the following day, west of the Standard Wagon works at Heywood. Some (not all) of the track between Bury and Heywood was lifted, and in Bury the cutting between the Knowsley Street and Manchester Road overbridges was filled in.

The East Lancashire Railway Preservation Society has re-opened Bury Bolton Street station with trains to Ramsbottom from 25 July 1987. It is hoped to extend operations to Rawtenstall in 1991. A connection with the Manchester line was retained at Buckley Wells and this has been used for the occasional special train to and from BR as well as the transfer of rolling stock. With the conversion of the Bury–Manchester line to overhead electrification as part of the Bury–Altrincham 'Metrolink' system, on which only tramway-type rolling stock is permitted, this connection is no longer available. The ELRPS is therefore exploring the possibility of re-opening the line from Bury Bolton Street to Heywood in order to regain a link with BR. At Bury, however, a bridge has been built over the 'Metrolink' line instead of the previous crossing on the level. The east-north curve round to Bolton Street has been re-excavated.

At one time it was thought that the trackbed between Bolton, Bradley Fold and Radcliffe, including the iron viaducts, whose girders were renewed in 1880–1, would be re-used by a 25kV electric line (part of the 'Pic-Vic' project) for trains running from Bolton via Radcliffe to Manchester Victoria and under the city to Manchester Piccadilly. The scheme was shelved and the Windsor Link (already mentioned) was built instead. At Bolton and at Radcliffe embankments and underbridges have been removed, but the two iron viaducts still stand.

The LNWR Clifton Branch

On the morning of Tuesday 28 April 1953 at 0535, a pair of semi-detached houses in Temple Drive, Swinton near Manchester, suddenly collapsed into a crater and the end wall of another house fell outwards. The cause of this disaster, in which five lives were lost and which was the only one of its kind in British railway history, was a roof failure in Clifton Hall tunnel, 58ft (18m) below, resulting in the closure of the 3½ mile (5.6km) double-track branch from Patricroft to Molyneux Junction, Clifton.

The threat to its monopoly of Liverpool traffic by the proposed Liverpool & Bury Railway, just described, so alarmed the Liverpool & Manchester company that by way of opposition a connection was projected in 1844 from the Liverpool & Manchester at Patricroft near Eccles, through a tunnel under Swinton, and a bridge under the Manchester & Bolton Railway at Clifton, to join the Manchester, Bury & Rossendale Railway, then under construction, at Molyneux Junction. By this means the L&M hoped to block the Liverpool & Bury Bill and to capture the traffic between these places. (See map, page 9.)

There was no time to lose, and preparations were made hurriedly. The line was surveyed by Elias Dorning (1819–96) who later was engineer of the Lanchashire Union Railways and negotiator of the purchase of the Horwich Works site for the LYR. Edward Woods (1814–1903), engineer of the L&M, prepared the plan and section. Powers to construct the branch were obtained in the L&M Act of 1845, which also authorised the Edge Hill–Waterloo line in Liverpool.

The Clifton branch would be quite useless to Bolton and Wigan, and so the L&M was unable to prevent the Liverpool & Bury Bill receiving the Royal Assent only ten days later. Meanwhile, construction was proceeding on the Manchester, Bury & Rossendale which, on the same day as the L&M Act, changed its name to the East Lancashire Railway. By the time this had opened in September 1846, the L&M had also lost its identity, having in 1845 been absorbed by the Grand Junction

Railway, which in 1846 had become part of the LNWR. As already related, the Liverpool & Bury was absorbed by the Manchester & Leeds in 1846, the following year becoming the LYR, and it was opened in 1848.

The newly formed LNWR thus found itself saddled with the construction of the Clifton branch which it did not want, and with another four years to complete it. Tenders were invited in 1847 and the contract was awarded to George Pauling, who was just then embarking on the construction of the second Woodhead tunnel. The only work of any magnitude on the branch was Clifton Hall tunnel, 1298yd (1187m) through wet sand and marl. It was worked from eight shafts, which were afterwards filled in; it was the fourth from the south end which was to cause the disaster over a century later.

The completed line was opened in February 1850 and a service of passenger trains began, four daily from Liverpool to Bury or Newchurch beyond Rawtenstall, and two on Sundays. In the reverse direction there were seven on weekdays and two on Sundays. There were no intermediate stations on the branch. After only four months the service was withdrawn, a sufficient commentary on its limited usefulness. However, with the opening of the Bury 'Loco Loop' in 1899 the branch at last proved useful for LYR excursions between Yorkshire and North Wales. Coal traffic came from Clifton Hall sidings serving the Wheatsheaf colliery near Pendlebury. So the Clifton branch, projected in opposition to the LYR, ultimately served that system.

When the Eccles–Tyldesley line was opened in 1864 (Chapter 1), it crossed the Clifton branch on the flat, but in 1881 the Tyldesley line was widened and a bridge was built to carry the Clifton branch over, with 1 in 60 gradients at each end. At the same time the spur shown in Plate 9 was built to provide through running from Clifton to Eccles, but it was used only from 1884 to 1891. The Weaste branch from Eccles down to the Manchester Ship Canal which might have provided a purpose for it was not opened until 4 November 1895.

Clifton Hall tunnel was known locally as 'Black Harry' tunnel, apparently from a foreman on the work, an Irishman named Harry with a black beard. It gave endless trouble, with settlement over coal workings and with water seepage. It was closed in World War II and was used to store tank wagons of liquid chlorine for a nearby battery factory; it was re-opened in October 1947.

In April 1953 brickwork began falling from the roof 481yd (440m) from the south end and repairs were put in hand at once, but, because all the tunnel records had been lost in an air raid in 1940 and in a fire in 1952, no-one was aware that the bricks were falling from under an old shaft. Ribs were prepared at Gorton works from old rails but before they could be fitted the roof collapsed and the sand filling the shaft poured into the tunnel forming a cavity and partial vacuum beneath the houses, causing their immediate and violent collapse.

It was decided not to re-open the line and it was abandoned from Clifton Hall sidings to Patricroft and the tunnel was filled in. With the closure of the Wheatsheaf colliery on 16 June 1961 the remainder of the line was closed. The last train was a brake van special from Patricroft over the remaining half-mile of track at that end, on 16 March 1963, with 0–6–0 tank No 47378.

Rochdale–Bacup

It was mentioned in the introduction how some branches were built in the full knowledge that they would not pay, and against opposition from many of the company's directors, simply to keep another company out of the district. The LYR from Rochdale to Bacup was such a line, promoted in 1860–2 against bitter opposition from within the company because of a threatened invasion by the MS&L and driven through at vast expense against formidable physical difficulties. A large viaduct at Rochdale gave endless trouble. Beyond Wardleworth the line became single. Construction was delayed by landslides and it was 1870 before the railway was opened to Facit, 5½ miles (8.8km), for passenger traffic. The double-track extension to Bacup over the highest summit on the LYR system, 965ft (294m), was completed in 1881. (See map, page 37 and Plate 10.)

As predicted, traffic was disappointing; with competition from electric trams and later from buses passenger receipts dwindled, yet it survived until 1947. Goods trains continued from Rochdale to Facit until 1963 and to Whitworth until 1967, after which the line was closed entirely.

The viaduct at Rochdale was demolished, but the magnificent stone viaduct over Healey Dell, 105ft (32m) high, remains, together with some interesting sections. Just south of Healey Dell viaduct is a curious 'double bridge'. The original one with approach embankments slid down the hill slope during construction and a new bridge had to be built closer to the hillside. Despite destruction of some of the trackbed under building development, much remains to interest the explorer.

Blackburn–Padiham–Rose Grove

The North Lancashire Loop was projected and built by the LYR to provide rail facilities at the small mill towns of Great Harwood and Padiham north of Accrington. Its 9 miles (14.5km) formed one of the most difficult and expensive sections of the LYR, taking five years to build. The Padiham–Rose Grove section was opened to goods traffic in 1875 and to passengers in 1876, but the Great Harwood section presented formidable difficulties with unstable earthworks and it was 1877 before it was opened throughout. Passenger trains ran between Blackburn and Burnley, taking about half an hour; the distance was about the same as that via Accrington.

Passenger and freight services were of a routine pattern, with occasional through trains routed that way to avoid

Plates 5 and 6. Above: Great Northern Railway Deansgate goods station, Manchester, about the turn of the century, with then new Ivatt 0–6–0 saddle tank shunting wagons into the warehouse. One of the ramps leading down to the ground-level lines is on the left. The yard is now a car park. On the right is the now-demolished Cheshire Lines goods warehouse, adjoining Central station. *Below*: Darcy Lever Viaduct on the Bolton–Bury line. When built in 1848 this and the nearby Burnden Viaduct were the first wrought-iron lattice-girder spans. The girders were renewed in 1880–1. In the foreground is the Manchester, Bolton & Bury Canal, (*From an old print in Bolton Museum and Art Gallery*)

Plates 7 and 8. Above: Bury train emerging from Thrutch tunnel on the former ELR Bacup branch, on 26 July 1962. On the left is Newchurch No 1 tunnel, 162yd long. Below: Looking up the 1 in 45 Baxenden bank from Accrington station on 20 June 1960. Stopping train to Manchester behind a Fairburn 2–6–4 tank about to leave. (John Marshall)

Accrington. In 1957 passenger trains were withdrawn, and after total closure between Great Harwood Junction, Blackburn, and Padiham in 1964 the track was lifted. From Rose Grove it is still used to serve Padiham power station.

Beyond Great Harwood the bleak moorland scenery gives way to more interesting country in the valley of the Lancashire Calder which is crossed by Martholme viaduct, a fine stone structure. This section of the track is worth exploring, and it has the added attraction of being close to places of great historical interest, such as Gawthorpe Hall (National Trust) at Padiham, and Whalley Abbey.

Standedge old tunnels and Micklehurst Loop

The circuitous route of the Manchester & Leeds left the way open for a more direct line passing through Huddersfield and Dewsbury. In 1844–5 both the MS&L and the Manchester & Leeds were building branches to Stalybridge, then on the boundary between Lancashire and Cheshire. (It became wholly in Cheshire in 1894.) The MS&L branch from Guide Bridge was opened on 23 December 1845 and the M&L branch from Miles Platting was opened to Ashton on 13 April and to Stalybridge on 15 October 1846.

Stalybridge was a good jumping-off point for a line to Huddersfield and Leeds, which would follow the course of the Huddersfield Canal up the Tame valley, through a tunnel under Standedge, and then down the Colne valley to Huddersfield. Two railway companies obtained Acts in 1845 to construct a new main line: the Leeds, Dewsbury & Manchester from Leeds via Dewsbury to join the Manchester & Leeds main line at Ravensthorpe, and the Huddersfield & Manchester Railway & Canal Co from the Manchester & Leeds at Heaton Lodge to Huddersfield and Stalybridge, with a branch to Delph. Both companies were amalgamated with the LNWR by an Act in 1847.

Standedge Tunnel under the Pennine watershed was 3 miles

66yd (4887m) long. The Huddersfield Canal, vested in the company under Section 50 of the 1845 Act, had already tunnelled through here in 1811, and the single-line railway tunnel was bored alongside to the south-east, using adits to the canal tunnel for access and removal of spoil. The railway was opened throughout on 1 August 1849, trains running via the LYR Stalybridge branch so as to connect with Liverpool trains at Victoria, although on the same day the Manchester South Junction line opened, giving a connection between London Road station and the Liverpool & Manchester, so that trains could equally well have used the MS&L Stalybridge branch. Trains still use the former LYR branch.

The single-line Standedge tunnel was a restriction, so in 1871 a second single-line bore was opened alongside, connected to the 1849 tunnel by adits. (See photograph, Plate 11.) Being the only level stretch of line on the entire route, water troughs were installed inside the tunnels at the Diggle or south ends in or before 1878. They were probably the only water troughs inside tunnels. In the centre a full size cross-bore connected the two single-line tunnels and in its centre was a platelayers' standard brick shed with roof, window and chimney, 1½ miles from the open air. The ribbed vaulting at the intersections, with its resemblance to ecclesiastical architecture, led to this being called 'the cathedral'.

In 1885, as part of the quadrupling of the entire LNWR route to Leeds, a new double-track loop was brought into use between Stalybridge and the south end of Standedge tunnels at Diggle, and also a new station at Stalybridge. Leaving Stalybridge New tunnel, 572yd (523m), the line crossed the Tame and then used the other side of the valley, opposite the original line. North of Micklehurst was a short tunnel under a road, and beyond Saddleworth was the Butterhouse tunnel, 329yd (301m). There were also several low viaducts. Passenger traffic began on 3 May 1886 and served four stations: Staley & Millbrook, Micklehurst, Friezland, and Uppermill. (See map opposite.)

To complete the four-tracking through to Huddersfield a

new double-track tunnel was bored under Standedge, on the north-west side of the canal tunnel, and brought into use on 5 August 1894. Through traffic tended to use the Micklehurst Loop and the old single-line tunnels, and this continued until the loop was closed in 1964. Freight traffic continued to work from Stalybridge to Friezland until 1965, and a single line was left in after that to serve the power station near Millbrook until 1975. The old single-line Standedge tunnels were closed in October 1966.

Branches to Delph and Oldham

The Huddersfield & Manchester Railway & Canal Act of 1845 included powers for a branch to the tiny Pennine town of Delph to give rail access to local mills. Another Act of 1846

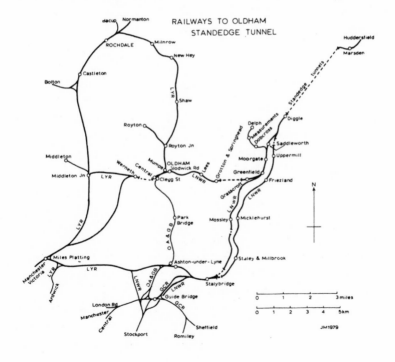

authorised a branch to Oldham, which was then served only by the steep branch from the Manchester & Leeds to Werneth.

The single-line Delph branch, barely 1½ miles (2.4km) long, was built first and was opened in 1851. Passenger services operated from Greenfield and, according to *Annals of Saddleworth 1200–1903* by Ammon Wrigley (1905), were provided by a single coach pulled by a horse, though this would involve the horse using the main line for a mile, for up to fifteen minutes. Six return journeys a day were operated. Apparently the pace was so slow that if passengers missed the 'train' they simply walked down the line and caught up with it. It became known as the 'Delph Donkey', a name which lasted until the passenger service was withdrawn. According to the account the horse was occasionally 'stowed' which suggests it rode on a wagon down the branch. Steam trains began in 1856 when the Oldham branch was opened. On 1 January 1912 motor-trains were introduced and a halt was opened on the branch at Dobcross. Another halt, named Measurements after the nearby mill, was opened on 18 March 1932.

On the Oldham branch the main work was Lydgate tunnel, 1332yd (1218m). The chief engineers were Locke and Errington, and the resident engineer James Grant Fraser. It was worked from five shafts of which one was filled-in after completion in February 1855; the deepest was No 2 from the Oldham end, 240ft (73m) deep. The tunnel was straight for 1046yd (956m) and on a 74-chain (1489m) radius curve for 286yd (261m).

The branch turned away westwards from the south end of Greenfield station and climbed through Lydgate tunnel at 1 in 100 to Grotton from where it dropped to Oldham, passing stations at Grotton & Springhead, and Lees where later there was a locomotive depot. At Oldham the line terminated at a temporary station at Mumps, beside the LYR station which had been open since 1 November 1847.

From the opening in 1856 many trains ran through from Oldham to Delph, and from 1 July 1862 the service was extended to Oldham Clegg Street on the line to Guide Bridge, dealt with later. The temporary station at Mumps was replaced by Glodwick Road station on 1 November 1862. With the introduction of the motor-trains in 1912 a halt was opened at Grasscroft between Greenfield and the tunnel, and the service was increased to thirty-six trains each way between Oldham and Greenfield and nineteen through to Delph. This increased service resulted in the spread of the Oldham residential district and a heavy commuter traffic which in due course gave rise to the road competition which eventually killed the line. Passenger trains on the Oldham and Delph branches were withdrawn in 1955. Goods trains continued to Delph until 1963 and between Oldham and Greenfield until 12 April 1964, on which date Lees shed also closed. The last freight train on 10 April, on which the author travelled, was pulled by Class 2 2–6–0 No 46452. (See Plate 12.) It ran from Oldham to Greenfield and down the main line to Mossley and back. From Greenfield the brake van was propelled to Oldham, giving an eerie and windy ride through Lydgate tunnel.

Oldham, Ashton-under-Lyne & Guide Bridge Junction Railway

The railway which became known as the Oldham, Ashton & Guide Bridge was originally conceived as part of a system of lines included in the Oldham Alliance Railway Company's Act of 1847 which authorised the Oldham Mumps–Ashton-under-Lyne–Guide Bridge; Mumps–Rochdale; a branch to Royton; and the Werneth–Miles Platting lines, all of which were built but under other Acts.

The OA&GB was eventually promoted in conjunction with the MS&L and the LNWR, and the company was incorporated in 1857. The line was in two portions, from a junction with the LNWR branch from Greenfield at Mumps to a junction with the LYR Stalybridge branch at Ashton and from another junction with this line to the MS&L at Guide Bridge.

The main station at Oldham was Clegg Street, close to the

LYR Central station. It was rebuilt in 1900, becoming the largest of the five stations at Oldham with a main platform 270ft (82m) long, a bay at the Ashton end, and an island platform, covered by an all-over roof. It was the only station at Oldham to boast a refreshment room. (See Plate 13.)

There was a curious cotton warehouse at Clegg Street, built by the LNWR. To fit on to the site it had to be built on a curved plan. One end was almost at right angles to the other. Between Glodwick Road and Clegg Street the OA&GB ran alongside the LYR, and a junction was put in enabling traffic to be interchanged.

At Park Bridge the Medlock was crossed by a stone viaduct 200yd (183m) long, 96ft 6in (29.4m) high with nine arches of 50ft (15.2m), and three of 23ft (7m), the latter filled in by the embankment. Intermediate stations were at Park Bridge and Ashton Oldham Road. The southern portion made Y junctions with both the LYR and the MS&L. Both portions were opened for passenger trains in 1861 and for goods in 1863.

In 1864 Isaac Watt Boulton had a siding laid in from the southern portion to serve his works, immortalised by A. R. Bennett in *The Chronicles of Boulton's Siding*. Many of his rebuilt locomotives were tried out on the OA&GB, including an 0–6–0 saddle tank rebuilt from one of Sturrock's steam tenders from the GNR. The siding works were disposed of in 1898 and Boulton died in 1899.

Until 1872 trains were operated by the MS&L. The LNWR took over some services in 1869–70 and from 1873 coaches were supplied jointly by both companies. The first passenger services consisted of nine trains from Oldham to Guide Bridge, two to Manchester London Road, eight from Guide Bridge to Oldham, and one from Manchester. On Sundays there were three to Guide Bridge and two to Manchester, four from Guide Bridge, and one from Manchester. The direct service to Manchester was subjected to numerous alterations, and in 1909 there was a service to and from Manchester Central.

From 16 September 1861 the OA&GB operated an omnibus

service between Oldham and Rochdale, but with the opening of the LYR line between these places in 1863 it was discontinued. The new LYR route made possible a through service between Rochdale, Oldham and London (King's Cross), taking over six hours. There were also trains between Oldham and Stalybridge, and to Marple and Macclesfield via the MS&L/North Staffordshire joint line opened in 1869.

Early services were worked by MS&L locomotives, mostly Sacré 2–4–0s and 2–4–0 well tanks. Parker 2–4–2 tanks appeared in 1889, and from 1893 these operated nearly all the services until replaced by the Robinson 4–4–2 tanks. It was one of these, C13 No 67417, which worked the last passenger train from Oldham to Guide Bridge on 2 May 1959.

LNWR trains to and from Stockport were at first worked by Webb 2–4–2 tanks and various Ramsbottom and Webb 0–6–0s. In LMS days LYR 0–6–0s became common, and later the Guide Bridge–Oldham–Greenfield–Delph services became a means of relieving other lines of some of the Fowler 2–6–2 tanks.

With the establishment of electric tram services in the early 1900s the OA&GB lost much of its local traffic, but passenger services survived both wars. With the closure of Glodwick Road station on 2 May 1955 at the end of the Greenfield and Delph services the OA&GB trains terminated at Clegg Street until withdrawn in 1959.

Park Bridge viaduct was reconstructed in 1960 and the line continued to handle a heavy parcels traffic to Clegg Street. This continued on the OA&GB until 1967, when the Oldham–Ashton section was closed completely. In 1970 it was dismantled. Park Bridge viaduct was demolished in February and March 1971. The southern section is still in use, though the 'Canal Curve', or west–north link, at Guide Bridge was taken up in June 1938. The parcels concentration depot of Oldham (1960) was closed in May 1981.

CHAPTER 3

Merseyside

Liverpool: Edge Hill to Crown Street and Wapping

When the Liverpool & Manchester Railway was opened in 1830 the Liverpool passenger terminus was in Crown Street, quite a distance from the commercial heart of the city, necessitating a service of horse omnibuses to connect with the trains. Crown Street remained the passenger terminus until completion of the extension down through a 2025yd (1852m) tunnel from Edge Hill to a new terminus at Lime Street, opened on 15 August 1836. On the same day Crown Street was closed to passengers and was used as a coal depot. The original single-line tunnel to the station, too small for locomotives, remained in use for wagon traffic which had to be hauled by horses.

In 1845 powers were obtained to extend an 80ft (24m) blind tunnel to form a through full size double-track tunnel 124yd (113m) long, leading into a cutting, on the south side of Wapping tunnel, and this was completed about 1846. Crown Street yard was further extended under an Act of 1868. The little that remained of the 1830 terminus at Crown Street was lost in an air raid in World War II, but the terminal yard was used as a coal depot until 1972. It has now been grassed over and planted with trees.

The goods terminal of the L&M was sited down by Wapping dock. To reach this a double-track tunnel 1 mile 490yd (2057m) long was bored from Edge Hill. The Liverpool sandstone was ideal for tunnelling, and in eighteen months the tunnel was finished. It was 'opened' on 7 June 1828, at the time the world's longest railway tunnel and the first for double-track. Its great size, 22ft (6.7m) wide and 16ft (4.9m) high, made it one of the

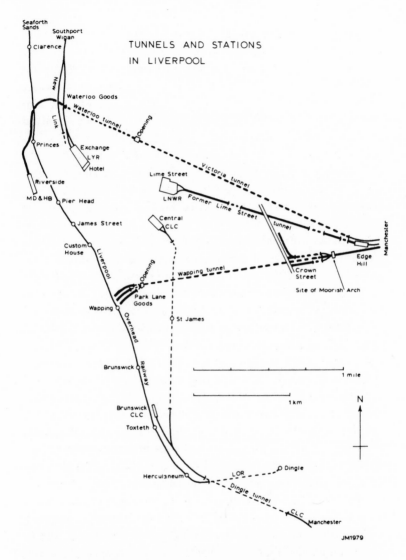

TUNNELS AND STATIONS
IN LIVERPOOL

Seaforth Sands
Southport Wigan
Clarence
New Link
Waterloo Goods
Waterloo tunnel
Opening
Princes
Exchange
LYR
Hotel
Riverside
MD&HB
Pier Head
James Street
Custom House
Liverpool
Central CLC
Lime Street
LNWR Former Lime Street
Victoria tunnel
tunnel
Manchester
Edge Hill
Crown Street
Site of Moorish Arch
Opening
Wapping tunnel
Park Lane Goods
Wapping
Overhead Railway
St James
Brunswick
1 mile
1 km
N
Brunswick CLC
Toxteth
Herculaneum
LOR
Dingle
Dingle tunnel
CLC
Manchester

JM1979

sights of Liverpool. In 1829 the roof was whitewashed and gas lights were installed every 50yd (45.7m), increased later to every 25yd. As the rest of the railway was far from ready the tunnel was opened for visitors at a shilling a time. In August the tunnel walls were whitewashed 'to the ground'. Shortly afterwards the composer Felix Mendelssohn, returning from

61

Scotland, visited the tunnel and on 25 August 1829 he wrote from Llangollen to his father, saying how, to fill in the time in Liverpool, he visited the railway and walked into Wapping tunnel but was rather nervous at not being able to see right through. However, he spoke to a workman and persuaded him to take him on a trolley through to the Mersey. They set off at 15mph down through the tunnel, gradually reaching an alarming speed. There were two headlamps but the draught blew them out. It became completely dark and Mendelssohn says how he saw nothing for the first time in his life. Half way down they passed a coal fire and the workman stopped and relit the lamps. He also comments on the extreme cold and on how relieved he was when they emerged safely into the warm daylight. But he found it an invigorating and satisfying experience. It can be claimed that Mendelssohn was the L&M's first passenger. On 21 August 1829, when it was visited by William Huskisson, about 3,000 people paid to see it. The tunnel lay on a gradient of 1 in 48 for 1980yd (1811m) from the Edge Hill end which necessitated rope haulage from a winding engine installed in the Moorish Arch at Edge Hill. Despite its early completion, traffic through the tunnel did not begin until December 1830.

The artist Thomas Talbot Bury (1811–77) produced a coloured aquatint inside the lower end and it was published by Ackermann, but it wrongly showed a train with a locomotive. A second version was produced in which the locomotive was disguised as a wagon, and haulage ropes were shown, but it still showed the large front wheels of the locomotive. In a third version the locomotive was completely changed into a wagon.

Wapping goods station was enlarged on the north side to cope with increasing traffic, and in 1864 a connecting line was authorised to give direct access. This involved making an opening at the bottom of Wapping tunnel in which to install a junction, the length of the tunnel being reduced to 1 mile 351yd (1930m). The lower end became a separate tunnel of 112yd (102m). The connecting line passed through a tunnel 77yd (70m) long. (See Plate 14.) In 1872 a further connection was authorised into an extension of the goods yard on the south side, involving brick arches under two streets, and this was completed in 1874. Plate 14 was taken from about the same viewpoint as the Bury picture, with which it should be compared.

Rope haulage through Wapping tunnel ended on 11 May 1896; from that date ascending trains were hauled by locomotives and descending trains were controlled by special 'Wapping tunnel brake vans'. Smoke soon made operation hazardous so in 1897–9 five ventilating shafts were made, one in the middle of Crown Street yard. After World War II shipping at the south docks declined until they were closed, while traffic to the Park Lane goods station at Wapping fell off until in 1965 the yard was closed and dismantled.

Edge Hill to Waterloo and Riverside station

The monopoly of Liverpool rail traffic by the L&M for eighteen years, from 1830–48, has been mentioned. Under the threat of invasion by the Liverpool & Bury Railway, the L&M obtained an Act in 1845 authorising, in addition to the Patricroft–Clifton line already described, and the new Crown Street tunnel, a new line from Edge Hill to the Mersey at Waterloo Road. This involved construction of over two miles of double-track tunnel: Victoria tunnel 1 mile 946yd (2474m) and, after a gap of a few yards, Waterloo tunnel 852yd (779m). It was opened on 1 August 1849.

Immediately beyond the end of Waterloo tunnel the line was crossed by two bridges carrying the LYR extension of Great Howard Street station, first a cast-iron bridge carrying goods lines and then a brick arch with a span of 150ft (45.7m). Today this carries the Merseyrail Link trains at the head of their steep descent into Moorfield tunnel. A large goods station was established fronting on to Waterloo Road opposite Victoria Dock. It was opened in 1849 and was enlarged in 1873–4.

By 1893 Southampton had begun to rival Liverpool for the

trans-Atlantic traffic. At Southampton trains could meet the liners and carry passengers directly to or from London. At Liverpool passengers had to be conveyed to and from Lime Street station by horse omnibuses, and timings depended on tides. This was a matter of concern to the Mersey Docks & Harbour Board and Liverpool Corporation as well as the LNWR, and when a boat load of Scandinavian immigrants bound for America was transferred from Hull to Southampton instead of to Liverpool something had to be done. Most urgent was the dredging of the bar at the mouth of the Mersey to permit the largest liners to enter at all states of the tide, and this went ahead with vigour. To give access to Princes Landing Stage for passenger trains the LNWR made a route through the Waterloo goods yard, while the MD&HB built a passenger terminal on Princes Pier, and named it Riverside. (See Plate 15.)

The opening of the new station and approach line was timed to coincide with the departure of the White Star steamer *Germanic* and the arrival of the Cunard *Catalonia* and the White Star *Teutonic* on 12 June 1895. The official opening ceremony was on 10 July. During the two world wars Riverside station was much used by troop trains. After World War II, with the main trans-Atlantic passenger traffic using Southampton, and other traffic declining with increasing use of air services, Riverside station fell into disuse. The last train left on 25 February 1971. Waterloo Dock goods station had already been closed in 1963.

Liverpool Exchange Station

The second railway to enter Liverpool, the Liverpool & Bury from Wigan, entered from the north-east and terminated alongside Great Howard Street just north of the Borough Gaol. Its opening in November 1848 ended the eighteen-year monopoly held by the Liverpool & Manchester. The section from Walton Junction to Liverpool was built jointly by the LYR and East Lancashire Railway whose line from Preston was then nearing completion. By the time this was opened in April 1849 the railway was being extended to a new terminus fronting on to Tithebarn Street. The extension involved crossing the new LNWR Edge Hill–Waterloo branch by a brick arch with a span of 150ft (45.7m) and climbing partly on lattice-girder bridges into the new station which stood on a brick viaduct 25ft (7.6m) above Tithebarn Street. It was a handsome building, opened on 13 May 1850, and renamed Exchange about 1855. With only five platform faces it soon proved inadequate for the traffic now coming in from Manchester, Bury, Preston and Southport, but its position on a viaduct made extension difficult.

After protracted arguments, and even a design competition, it was decided in 1882 to demolish the entire station and to build a new one at a lower level, involving alterations to canal basins and streets, and a large hotel on Tithebarn Street forming a frontage to the station. The architect Henry Shelmadine designed the buildings in pretentious Victorian style, and work began in 1884. The new station was partly opened in 1886 and completely in 1888. It had ten platform faces under a ridged roof of three spans which, with its iron columns, gave an air of elegance and spaciousness unique on the LYR. The hotel, opened on 13 August 1888, was one of the most luxurious in Liverpool.

The station became exceedingly busy, with expresses to and from Manchester and Yorkshire, Preston and the north, and heavy local traffic to Ormskirk and Southport. Electrification to Southport was completed in 1904 and to Ormskirk in 1913. Traffic continued at high density until the 1960s when rationalisation of Liverpool–Manchester and Yorkshire services reduced the number of long-distance trains. Completion of the electrification from Crewe to Preston in 1974 ended through services between Exchange and Preston. Trains now terminated at Ormskirk, with a separate service from there to Preston.

The end came with the opening of the 'Link' line of the new Merseyrail system on 2 May 1977. The remaining trains, all now electric, were re-routed via the former Great Howard Street line over the great arch across the former LNWR and down a steep gradient into a tunnel under Exchange Station. Exchange

Station itself was closed entirely on 30 April 1977, together with the approach viaducts from Exchange Junction.

Liverpool Central Station

Central Station formed the Liverpool terminus of the Cheshire Lines Railway from Manchester. A brief outline of the formation of the CLC was given in the section on Manchester Central. The through route from Manchester was completed in 1873, but the portion from Garston to Liverpool was opened on 1 June 1864, terminating at Brunswick in the south docks area. To bring trains into the centre of Liverpool a new station was planned on Ranelagh Street; the extension from Brunswick was authorised only eight weeks after the Brunswick terminus was opened, but it took ten years to complete it. It involved about a mile of tunnelling, and an intermediate station, St James (closed on 1 January 1917). The tunnel between St James and Central cut through the arch of the LNWR Wapping tunnel and the CLC trains were carried across on iron girders.

The terminus, named Central (Plate 16), had an arched roof 65ft (19.8m) high. It was opened in March 1874 and in May became the terminus of the CLC service to and from Manchester London Road. When the CLC established its own terminus in Manchester in 1877 the service became better than that provided by the LNWR and LYR, trains running via Warrington in 45 min. For many years the CLC provided the principal service between Liverpool and Manchester, and the most punctual. At its busiest period the CLC was handling trains to Manchester, Stockport, Aintree and Southport.

An important development in the history of Liverpool Central was the opening of the Mersey Railway to Central Low Level on 11 January 1892, but traffic by this route did not develop greatly until the Mersey Railway was electrified in 1903. The intended connection with the CLC was not completed until 1978, as part of the new Merseyrail Link.

Central Station had by then been closed. On 5 September

1966, the Manchester service was transferred to Lime Street; but the Central–Gateacre service remained until final closure of Central in 1972. The station was then completely demolished. With the tunnel now free, the Merseyrail Link was extended from Central Low Level and brought up into the CLC tunnel. The century-old iron girders across Wapping Tunnel were replaced by concrete beams. From 3 January 1978 trains began running to Garston from the Southport, Ormskirk and Kirkby lines.

CLC North Liverpool Lines

Although the CLC had established its connection with the Liverpool dock system at Brunswick in 1864, this was at the extreme south end of the docks and placed the owning companies in a disadvantageous position compared with the LNWR and LYR, which by that time had good connections to the dock lines farther north where the system had expanded during the 1850s. To open up access to the northern docks, in 1873 the CLC acquired 23 acres for a station close to the Sandon (1851) and Huskisson (1852) docks. It was 1½ miles (2.4km) in a direct line from Central station, but to reach it from there would have meant another long and expensive tunnel under Liverpool. To avoid this, a route was planned from the main line at Hunts Cross and Halewood, round the east of Liverpool, approaching Huskisson station from the north via Walton on the Hill. Powers were obtained in the CLC Act of 1874. The scheme included an extension from Fazakerley to join the LYR north of Aintree. Work began in 1875 and the lines were opened from Hunts Cross and Halewood to Aintree for all traffic and to Walton on the Hill for freight in December 1879. The extension through the tunnels from Walton on the Hill to Huskisson was opened for goods in July 1880. (See map, page 79.) A locomotive depot was established at Walton on the Hill.

A curious feature of this section could be seen where it emerged from the tunnel beside the LYR Kirkdale station, immediately to be carried over the LNWR Canada Dock branch by a girder bridge. This was a second tunnel entrance to the east of the running tunnel, penetrating about 150yd and coming to a blind end, possibly for future quadrupling. Farther south, the line passed beneath a substantial aqueduct built to carry the Leeds & Liverpool Canal.

In August 1880 a passenger service began to Huskisson, but it ran for less than five years, after which it was terminated at Walton on the Hill until withdrawn at the end of 1917.

The Midland Railway goods station at Sandon Dock was reached in November 1882 by a link from Huskisson under the LYR at its Sandhills station. To gain access to the Huskisson and Sandon goods stations from the north, the Midland negotiated running powers over the LYR from Hellifield to Liverpool via Blackburn by an agreement on 26 November 1884, and Midland freight trains began running by this route on 1 August 1888. The Midland took further advantage of the north Liverpool lines in 1885 when it opened its goods line from the CLC at Fazakerley to Alexandra Dock, which had been opened on 3 December 1880.

With its footing well established in north Liverpool, the Cheshire lines captured a good share of the docks traffic. The Aintree line became busy on race days while Gateacre handled heavy suburban traffic. In 1884 the Southport & Cheshire Lines Extension (next chapter) continued the line from Aintree to Southport and brought additional passenger traffic, particularly in summer. Gateacre became the terminus of CLC suburban trains from Liverpool Central; although the journey of 9¼ miles (15km) was circuitous compared with the direct distance of 7 miles (11km) the time of about 25 min remained competitive to the end of the service in 1972. The number of trains declined with the closure of the Southport extension in 1952. Passenger trains to Aintree continued until November 1960 when the service was cut back to Gateacre.

Traffic at Huskisson declined during the 1950s and 1960s, along with rail traffic to all the Mersey docks, and it ended on 1 January 1969 when the station was transferred to National

Plates 9 and 10. *Above*: Looking north across the bridge carrying the LNWR Clifton branch over the Eccles–Tyldesley line near Patricroft, on 16 March 1963. The bridge was built in 1881 to replace an earlier flat crossing on the left. On the right is the formation of the curve between the two lines, in use 1884–91. A Bolton–Manchester freight train is passing. Today the whole is obliterated by the M602 motorway. *Below*: Shawforth station on the Rochdale–Bacup line on 25 June 1960, looking towards Bacup. The station was closed on 16 June 1947. (*John Marshall*)

Plates 11 and 12. *Above*: Standedge old tunnels, 1849 on left, 1871 on right, from a Manchester–Leeds train at Diggle. The water troughs were installed just inside this end. *Below*: Class 2 2–6–0 No 46452 on the last goods train from Oldham to Greenfield and Mossley, passing Grotton & Springhead station on 10 April 1964. Lydgate tunnel beyond. (*John Marshall*)

Carriers Ltd, though the tracks were used for wagon storage for a while afterwards. The former Midland goods station at Alexandra (Langton) Dock remained open until 1970. With the closure of Knotty Ash to freight traffic on 1 May 1972 the entire north Liverpool line was closed and abandoned.

The Liverpool Overhead Railway

The Liverpool Overhead Railway was the outcome of the growth of the Liverpool dock system and the need for a passenger transport service which would not block road and rail entrances to the quays. The earliest docks were opened well before the railway age: Salthouse in 1753, King's, Queen's and Wapping before 1800. By the time the Liverpool & Manchester Railway was opened in 1830 Prince's and Clarence had been added. With the opening of the Huskisson group in 1852 the dock system extended along $3\frac{1}{2}$ miles (5.6km) of the Mersey.

In that year a scheme for a 4 mile (6.4km) overhead railway was put forward but was rejected. Further dock construction added the extensive Canada system in 1859, but it was not until 1878 that the MD&HB applied for powers for a $5\frac{1}{4}$mile (8.5km) elevated single-line steam railway which was rejected by the Board of Trade.

A new period of dock construction began in the 1880s, to cater for larger steamships, and by 1884 the system extended from Herculaneum in the south to Hornby in the north, $5\frac{1}{2}$ miles (8.8km). In 1882 the MD&HB obtained powers for a double-track overhead railway 6 miles (9.6km) long, but nothing was started and in 1887 the Liverpool Overhead Railway Company was formed to build the railway, obtaining an Act in 1888. Sir Douglas Fox and J. H. Greathead were appointed engineers. A further Act in 1892 authorised a northern extension to Seaforth Sands and a southern extension through an 800yd (732m) tunnel to Dingle. (See Plate 18.)

The overhead structure consisted of wrought-iron girders on columns with a standard span of 50ft (15.24m), giving a clearance of 16ft (4.877m) above the road. With its opening in 1893–6 it became the world's first electric overhead railway. Multiple-unit trains operated on a 500V dc third-rail system. In 1905 the LYR opened a connection to the LOR from its newly-electrified Liverpool–Southport line at Seaforth, and in 1906 began a through service between Southport and Dingle using special light-weight cars. This service was withdrawn in World War I.

The average distance between stations was 715yd (654m). The train service varied between one every 2 minutes at busy times to one every 10 minutes, and between the wars was carrying up to 15 million passengers a year. Although advertisements claimed that the LOR gave an unrivalled view of the docks and ships, in fact the traveller saw little more than the backs of warehouses for much of the journey.

Heavy damage in air raids in 1940–1 was quickly repaired and in 1944 the railway carried 14 million passengers. In 1956 this had fallen to 10 million, and by that time extensive decking renewals had become necessary at a cost of £2 million. Neither the MD&HB nor Liverpool Corporation would take-over the line, so at the end of 1956 it was closed and dismantled. There is no doubt that falling traffic would have forced its closure before much longer; today, with most of the southern docks closed, the traffic scarcely exists.

Wirral Railway–Seacombe Branch

The entire route length of the Wirral Railway was 13 miles (21km), so that this tiny branch, only 2¼ miles (3.6km) long, represented a substantial part of the system of which it formed the eastern extremity. It connected at Seacombe landing stage with the Mersey ferry to and from Liverpool, giving a journey time from Liverpool to West Kirby of 33 minutes. It also served as the northern extremity of the joint Great Central and Wrexham, Mold & Connah's Quay Railway. This line, from Bidston to the GCR near Connah's Quay, was originally authorised as part of the Wirral Railway by a Certificate of 1883, but it was transferred to the joint companies in 1889.

The Seacombe branch was authorised in 1881 as an extension of the Hoylake & Birkenhead Rail & Tramway Company's line which, under the same Act, changed its name to the Seacombe, Hoylake & Dee Side Railway. The tramway had been transferred to Birkenhead Tramways in 1879. The railway was amalgamated with the Wirral Railway in 1891, and it was this company which built the double-track branch and opened it in 1895. There was one intermediate station, Liscard & Poulton,

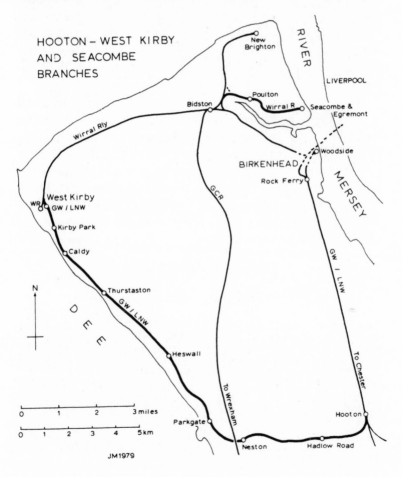

HOOTON – WEST KIRBY
AND SEACOMBE
BRANCHES

JM1979

1½ miles (2.4km) from Seacombe, at the summit of the branch. The ruling gradient was 1 in 100.

Passenger trains ran between Seacombe and West Kirby, providing a commuter service for north Wirral residents working in Liverpool. These were already served by the connection between the Wirral and Mersey Railways at Birkenhead Park established in 1888, but the 'open-air' route via Seacombe was greatly preferred to the Mersey tunnel in steam days. Not until this was electrified in 1903 did this route begin to draw off some of the Seacombe traffic.

The Bidston–Harwarden Bridge line of the MS&L/GCR /WM&CQR was opened in 1896 and its trains began operating to Seacombe in 1898 using running powers over the WR.

The Seacombe branch joined the Bidston–New Brighton line (opened 1888) at Seacombe Junction. An east-north curve was also built making possible through running between Seacombe and New Brighton, but this was closed in 1911 and taken up in 1916.

With electrification of the Wirral Railway in 1938 a through service of electric trains was established between Liverpool Central Low Level and West Kirby. Traffic on the Seacombe branch continued to decline and passenger trains were withdrawn in 1960.

Hooton–West Kirby

This was the only example of a true country branch line in the Wirral. It began as a single-line branch of 4 miles 53 chains (7.5km) from Hooton, on the GWR/LNWR joint Birkenhead Railway, to Parkgate, opened in 1866. In the same year the Hoylake Railway, the earliest portion of what later became the Wirral Railway, opened its single line from Birkenhead to Hoylake, and also obtained powers to extend to Parkgate to provide rail access to the Deeside townships of Heswall and Neston. All that was built of this was the extension to West Kirby, opened in 1878.

Thus it was left for the Birkenhead Railway to complete the 7 miles 25 chains (11.76km) from Parkgate to West Kirby. Powers were obtained in 1882 and the extension was opened in 1886. At the same time a new station was opened at Parkgate.

Although all the over and under-bridges were built for double track, only a single line was laid. It served stations at Hadlow Road, Neston, Parkgate, Heswall and Thurstaston, with eleven trains each way on weekdays and four on Sundays. Stations were later opened at Caldy and Kirby Park between Thurstaston and West Kirby. The only through service from the Wirral Railway was a through coach between New Brighton and London Euston, via West Kirby, started in October 1923. There were no engineering features of note, apart from a rock cutting at Neston, but the railway provided a pleasant rural ride with attractive views over the Dee Estuary as it ran along the foot of the hills between Heswall and West Kirby. The trains were operated by both the LNWR and GWR. The same pattern of service continued to the end, except for the withdrawal of Sunday trains after World War II.

By this time passenger traffic was declining; Thurstaston, Caldy and Kirby Park stations were closed in 1954 and passenger trains over the line ended in September 1956. Goods trains continued to serve all the stations except Caldy, which never had goods facilities, until May 1962.

After closure, Cheshire County Council bought almost the whole trackbed, for development as a country walkway similar to the Tissington and High Peak trails in Derbyshire. With assistance from the Countryside Commission the old branch became the Wirral Country Park, opened in 1973, an enjoyable 12-mile walk through pleasant country and beside the Dee Estuary with views across to North Wales. On the site of Thurstaston station (238235) a visitor centre and car park have been established. At Hadlow Road station east of Neston one platform and a line of rails have been restored and the buildings renovated and fitted out as a museum of the typical country station and of the branch as a whole. This alone is worth a visit. It is shown in Plate 19.

CHAPTER 4

West Lancashire

The West Lancashire Railway: Southport–Preston

Southport, like Blackpool and Morecambe, owed its rapid growth to the railway. By 1855 it was well served by trains to and from Liverpool, Wigan and Manchester, and by the junction with the East Lancashire Railway at Burscough it had connection with Preston, albeit by an L-shaped route with reversal at Burscough. Between Southport and Preston lay a stretch of flat marshy country bordering the south side of the Ribble Estuary. The thinly spread population in scattered, sprawling villages, was mainly concerned with agriculture, and it is not surprising that early schemes to build a railway between the two towns failed in Parliament because it was considered that the district would not provide sufficient traffic.

However, under the title of 'The West Lancashire Railway Company' a Bill for a railway, with a separate station at Preston to avoid over-crowding the North Union station, received the Royal Assent in 1871. This was only the beginning of the company's troubles. After work had at last begun in 1873 the contractor failed and threatened collapse was just avoided by an arrangement with Baron Albert Grant, financier and company promoter of doubtful reputation. Lack of capital still retarded progress and the company was not encouraged by the LYR which, to forestall competition, opened a north-to-west curve between the Southport and Preston lines at Burscough in 1878 to permit through running. No through service was put on, and passengers still had to change at Burscough Junction.

In 1876 work began again under a new contractor who, by taking the then pioneering step of using a steam navvy, was able to have about 7½ miles (12km) of line, from Southport to the River Douglas at Hesketh Bank, ready for opening in 1878. But Hesketh Bank was no place for a railway terminus, surrounded by open country with a few houses, so the company obtained powers to operate steam vessels to a variety of places, including the Isle of Man. By extending the railway along the bank of the River Douglas to the Tarleton branch of the Leeds & Liverpool Canal it was possible for trains to and from Southport to connect with a steamboat service for Liverpool. Only minimal freight rates could make such a devious route competitive with the direct LYR line.

After further delays because of financial difficulties the remaining works were let to yet another contractor who was soon floundering about in sticky clay in Penwortham cutting. By using a large American steam navvy and several locomotives day and night to move half-a-million cubic yards of earth, the work was completed by 1882. The twenty-two bridges on this section included a swing bridge over the tidal River Douglas (where twenty-four iron cylinders had to be sunk 20ft into the bed of the river) and an iron bridge of five spans on stone piers across the Ribble at Preston.

Despite its poverty the company erected a pompous-looking terminal station at Southport, designed in Gothic style by Charles H. Driver of Westminster. The Preston terminus in lower Fishergate was less pretentious. The stations were still unfinished in September 1882 when the railway was inspected by Major General Hutchinson, but as it was Preston Guild week (an event occurring every twenty years), he permitted a service to be operated ten days before the official opening. The line was double-track throughout.

To extend the facilities offered by the WLR a connection was built in 1883 to join the former ELR 'Preston Extension' at what became Whitehouse South Junction. It involved constructing a bridge through the North Union embankment, under six tracks, without interrupting the NUR traffic. The soft ground made it an exceedingly difficult task. With its completion a through service began between Southport and Blackburn using running powers over the LYR. At first all the Blackburn trains called at Preston WLR station where they reversed. Out of a total of seventeen trains between Southport and Preston, ten ran through to Blackburn. Fast trains covered the 11½ miles (18.5km) in 21 min, with a stop at Bamber Bridge to set down from Preston and to pick up on the journey from Blackburn.

Traffic on the WLR never fulfilled the hopes of the promoters, and in 1886 the impoverished railway passed into the hands of a receiver. It struggled along for another 13 years until it was absorbed by the LYR in 1897. A curve was built on to the former ELR at Whitehouse North Junction giving direct access to Preston Joint station, and the WLR station was closed. From this period the Blackburn trains avoided Preston, so the number of trains between Southport and Preston was reduced. In 1910 there were fourteen daily trains each way between Southport and Preston and four to and from Blackburn.

When the LYR pioneered its electrification between Liver-pool and Southport it extended the electric services along the former WLR as far as Crossens, 3¼ miles (5.2km) out from Southport, and a fairly intensive local service was introduced which was of great value to the residential population on the north side of the town. This pattern of services lasted throughout the LMS period and World War II. In the 1950s when economies were being made on other lines with diesel trains, the WLR section carried on with Class 5 4–6–0s hauling lightly-loaded trains of three coaches stopping at fully-staffed stations, some of which lay considerable distances from the small villages they served. It was not surprising that the line succumbed in the period of Beeching closures, though it was regrettable that the well-used Crossens electric service was also withdrawn. It served a well-populated residential district with intermediate stations at Meols Cop, Hesketh Park and Churchtown, and was well used for business and shopping. To judge from the number of prams carried on the Crossens electrics, its closure must have involved many families in a changed pattern of life.

Today the traveller by rail between Southport and Preston

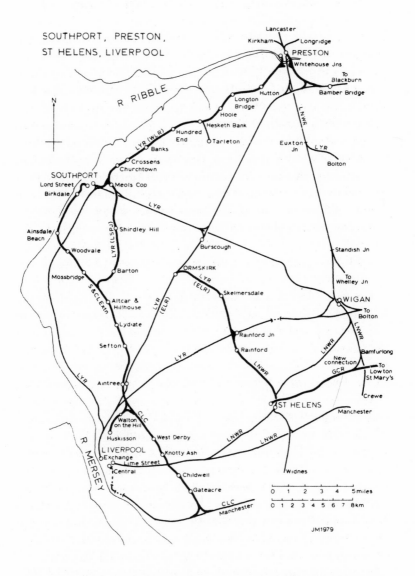

SOUTHPORT, PRESTON,
ST HELENS, LIVERPOOL

must again go via Burscough, but now with a half-mile walk
between Burscough Bridge on the Southport line and
Burscough Junction on the Ormskirk line.

The Southport & Cheshire Lines Extension Railway

Ask anyone to plot a route from Liverpool to Southport avoiding all major centres of population and it is likely that he will arrive at the line of the Southport & Cheshire Lines Extension Railway. The opening of the Cheshire Lines branch from Hunts Cross to Aintree on 1 December 1879 (Chapter 3), brought the CLC within striking distance of Southport. Despite their adequate rail services, people in Southport wanted to be connected to the Cheshire Lines, and in 1880 succeeded in persuading the CLC to extend the line from Aintree. For this purpose the Southport & Cheshire Lines Extension Railway Company was incorporated in 1881 with powers to build a line through the open country, passing between Formby and Ainsdale by a bridge over the LYR and following a route along the foot of the sand dunes to a magnificent terminus on Lord Street, Southport's main shopping thoroughfare. (See Plate 20.)

The 14½ mile double-track railway was opened in 1884 and a service of nine trains each way weekdays and three on Sundays was operated between Manchester Central and Southport. The fasts covered the 49½ miles (80km) in about 1hr 10min, compared with the 1 hour for the 35 miles (56km) via Bolton on the LYR. Connections for Liverpool were made at Gateacre. Trains were worked by MS&L, later GCR and LNER locomotives as on the CLC main system. During the LNER period from 1923 a wide variety of former GCR locomotives could be seen on the trains, from old Pollitt 0–6–0s of class J10 to D9 and Director 4–4–0s and various 4–6–0 classes. LNER classes included B17 and B1 4–6–0s and K3 2–6–0s, even occasionally a GER B12 4–6–0. The LMS was represented by class 4F 0–6–0s, 2P 4–4–0s and later by Ivatt 2–6–0s. It was the numerous excursions from far and wide that made the S&CLE popular, but most of these could be re-routed over the former LYR lines.

Its roundabout route and the sparsely-populated district through which it passed made the extension an early victim of the difficult times following World War II and all trains were withdrawn in 1952.

Liverpool, Southport & Preston Junction Railway

This railway, with a title out of proportion to its mere 7 miles (11km) of double-track route, was in effect a branch of the West Lancashire Railway from a triangular junction at Meols Cop to the Southport & Cheshire Lines Extension near Altcar. It was partly the outcome of an unsuccessful attempt by the WLR in 1882 to obtain powers for a connection in a tunnel to the Southport & Cheshire Lines Extension, then under construction, to give the WLR access to Liverpool. The LSPJ was an alternative means of achieving this and it was largely a WLR project under the name of a different company.

Despite the flat country it was not an easy line to build. The foundation of the bridge over the LYR at Blowick near Southport had to be carried down to a depth of 63ft (19.2m) below the LYR, and boggy ground made construction difficult in places.

When the LSPJ was opened in 1887 the S&CL Extension had been open for just three years. Trains ran between Southport and Altcar & Hillhouse, where they connected with trains on the S&CLE. No passenger trains ran direct from Preston avoiding Southport, so the LSPJ did not fulfil its purpose as a route from Preston to Liverpool except for freight traffic. The line passed through an even more sparsely-populated area than the S&CLE, and passengers were few.

In 1897, together with the WLR, it was absorbed by the LYR which saw no reason for sending Preston–Liverpool traffic by this route, so to compensate the S&CLE for loss of traffic it agreed to pay that company £1,500 per annum.

To reduce operating costs, in 1906 the LYR introduced a steam railmotor service between Southport and Altcar & Hillhouse and opened four new halts on the line. The railmotor became known as the 'Altcar Bob'. The passenger service survived until 1938, and goods trains continued until the S&CLE closed in 1952.

Garstang & Knott End Railway

Railway promoters in the 1860s and 1870s were great optimists. In 1864 a group obtained powers for a railway $11\frac{1}{2}$ miles (18.5km) long from the Lancaster–Preston line at Garstang & Catterall station, 9 miles (14.5km) north of Preston, passing through Garstang and Pilling to Knott End, adjoining the ferry across the Wyre estuary from Fleetwood. Apart from Garstang, a large village on the Lancaster Canal about two miles from the main line station, the railway passed through quiet farming country or peat bogs with no centres of population anywhere. Knott End was a tiny hamlet, while the town of Fleetwood was already well served by the Preston & Wyre Railway. In the flat country almost no earthworks were required, beyond low embankments each end of the girder bridge over the little River Wyre near Garstang and a shallow cutting beyond the girder bridge over the Lancaster Canal. With insufficient capital, the struggling company managed to complete its single line as far as Pilling in 1870 with 7 miles (11km) of rickety iron rails, 48lb/yd (23.8kg/m), attached direct to sleepers by coach screws. A locomotive, *Hebe*, was hired with some coaches and services began. When the locomotive needed overhauling in March 1872 services were suspended for two days. Soon after this *Hebe* was removed by its owners because the rent was unpaid. The company worked its traffic with a horse until an 0–4–0 tank *Union* was bought by debenture holders, and loco-motive-hauled traffic was resumed in 1875. Another locomotive, *Farmers Friend*, started work in 1876 but still traffic failed to make a profit, and in 1878 the railway was placed in the hands of a receiver. However, in 1890 it began to pay interest to deben-ture holders and by 1894 it had paid-off its debts.

In 1898 the newly formed Knot End (*sic*) Railway Company obtained powers to complete the line to Knott End as a light railway and to use the G&KER. The 4 mile (6.4km) extension was completed in 1908 and a passenger service began, with one train which started at Garstang at 0700, returned from Pilling at 0748, and then ran between the termini until it arrived at

Garstang from Pilling at 1850. The overall journey time was 35 to 40 minutes. Two new locomotives were obtained, 0–6–0 side tank *Knott End* and a 2–6–0 tank *Blackpool*. In 1920 the company hired a steam railmotor from the LNWR.

At the Grouping in 1923 the KER was the smallest constituent of the LMS. Passenger trains continued until 1930. From 1950–63 freight trains terminated at Pilling, after which they ran only to Garstang Town until this last section closed in 1965.

Preston & Longridge Railway

Stone from Longridge Fell, north-east of Preston, was quarried from about 1830, being used for many buildings in Preston and for Liverpool docks. To facilitate its transport to Preston, the Preston & Longridge Railway Company was incorporated in 1836 with powers to build a railway from St Paul's Square in Preston to Longridge. No heavy earthworks were required, yet the 6½ miles (10.5km) of single-line railway were not completed until March 1839, and even then more than a year passed before the line was opened. At first it was operated by horses, passenger trains running on Wednesdays and Saturdays. It was the first railway into Preston, apart from the Preston & Walton Summit Plateway mentioned below.

In 1846 the little P&LR became involved in a larger scheme to link Fleetwood with the Leeds & Bradford Railway between Skipton and Colne under the title of the Fleetwood, Preston & West Riding Junction Railway. All that was completed of this was a connection at Preston between the Preston & Wyre and Preston & Longridge Railways, much of it in cut-and-cover tunnels, opened in 1850. Apart from a short length of cutting and embankment near Hurst Green (682369), no further work was carried out and the powers lapsed.

Under Section 64 of the P&L Act, the company was forbidden to use locomotives or fixed engines without the consent of two justices of the peace. This consent must have been obtained in 1848 when, on 12 June, the first locomotive-hauled train on the P&L left Preston behind one named *Addison* after the chairman. In 1867 the whole undertaking was absorbed jointly by the LNWR and LYR.

In June 1868 a private branch was opened from Grimsargh to Whittingham mental hospital mainly for carriage of stores, but which also carried passengers free of charge. It was interesting because latterly one of the locomotives was a Stroudley D1 0-4-2 tank from Brighton. Passenger trains ran until 1957, although between Preston and Longridge the passenger service was withdrawn in 1930. Traffic from Longridge quarries ended during the 1950s but freight continued to Longridge until 1967. (See Plate 21.) The line is still used as far as the sidings serving Preston power station.

Preston & Walton Summit Plateway

This little line, only 4¾ miles (7.6km) long, is included because part of its track forms a pleasant walk near Preston. It was opened in 1803 to provide a connection across the Ribble valley between the north and south sections of the Lancaster Canal. John Rennie, engineer of the canal, designed a large aqueduct to carry the canal across the Ribble, but shortage of money resulted in the tramway connection being built instead.

It was a double-track 'plateway' with a gauge of 5ft 0in (1.524m) over the outsides of the plates. From the canal basin in Preston it passed under Fishergate in a tunnel which was later enlarged to form a road approach to the goods station. It then descended an incline of 1 in 6, worked by a Boulton & Watt engine and an endless chain, to the Ribble which it crossed on a wooden bridge. The replacement bridge, now carrying a footway, is still known as 'Tram Bridge'. A long embankment led to the foot of another incline from which the line ran across fields to the southern section of the canal at Walton Summit. The tramroad remained in use until 1859.

CHAPTER 5

Between Blackburn and St Helens

Lancashire Union Railways; Whelley Loop; LYR Hindley–Horwich

The area around Wigan was once one of the richest coalfields in England with some of the thickest seams. Much of the coal mined there in the mid-nineteenth century went to Liverpool for export, or to the various Lancashire textile towns to feed the boilers driving the hundreds of giant mills.

Liverpool was an expensive port, while rail routes from Wigan to the expanding towns of east Lancashire – Blackburn, Accrington, Burnley, Nelson and Colne – were indirect. In 1853 the LNWR opened a new dock at Garston on the upper Mersey, with good coal-handling facilities, and offering lower shipping charges, and the Wigan coal owners desired direct rail access there and to east Lancashire.

To meet this need the Lancashire Union Railways Company was formed in 1863 to build a system of lines connecting Blackburn, Wigan and St Helens. The LNWR gave it strong support, seeing it as a means of penetrating a stronghold of the LYR. The latter company was immediately alerted, putting forward a scheme of its own for railways from Blackburn to Chorley and Wigan.

After a long parliamentary struggle a scheme was evolved whereby the LYR line from Blackburn to Chorley would be built jointly by the LYR and LUR. The LYR would build a railway from Blackrod near Horwich, on the Bolton–Preston line, to Hindley on the Bolton–Wigan line, in connection with a short branch to Horwich, while the LUR would continue the route from the Bolton–Preston line at Adlington to join the North Union Railway just north of Wigan and a branch round the east of Wigan to the St Helens Canal & Railway system near St Helens, with a connection to the NUR south of Wigan, thus giving access to Widnes and Garston. These lines were authorised by two Acts in 1864. By another Act in 1865 the lines from Cherry Tree near Blackburn to Boar's Head Junction north of Wigan were vested jointly in the LYR and LUR.

Heavy earthworks were needed on the various sections. The Blackburn–Chorley line, 8½ miles (13.7km) included two embankments over 80ft (24.4m) high and a stone viaduct of nine spans crossing the Lancaster (Leeds & Liverpool) Canal at Botany Brow near Chorley. It was heavily graded, with long climbs at 1 in 60 to the summit at Brinscall, about half-way. From Cherry Tree Junction near Blackburn there were stations at Feniscowles, Withnell, Brinscall and Heapey.

The Adlington–Boar's Head section, 4 miles (6.4km), was also heavily graded, with a ruling gradient of 1 in 90 for about a mile above Red Rock station. The only other station, White Bear, was close to the junction at Adlington. Near Boar's Head the railway was carried across the deep Douglas Valley at a height of 86ft (26.2m) by a viaduct of seven wrought-iron spans. Between there and Red Rock the Lancaster Canal was carried over the line in a substantial aqueduct.

All sections were opened to goods and passengers during 1868–9. The LNWR, having absorbed the St Helens Railway in 1864, worked all passenger trains between St Helens and Wigan, and between Boar's Head and Adlington. Both the LNWR and the LYR worked the trains between Blackburn and Chorley, the LNWR trains then proceeding to Wigan via Boar's Head and the LYR via Hindley. A shuttle service on the short branch from Blackrod to Horwich began in 1870. For a brief period, from January to March 1872, there was a passenger service between St Helens and Whelley on the line round the east of Wigan. The station house at Whelley remained for nearly a century after closure.

In 1882 the LNWR opened a connection from the main line

Plates 13 and 14. Above: Remains of Clegg Street station, Oldham, looking north on 30 August 1965; Oldham, Ashton-under-Lyne & Guide Bridge Junction Railway. *Below*: Tunnels into Wapping goods station from the lower end of Wapping tunnel, on 10 January 1966. The viewpoint is about the same as the well-known lithograph of 1829 by T. T. Bury. The centre tunnel is the lower end of the original Liverpool & Manchester Railway tunnel. The opening to the right was made in 1864–5 and to the left in 1873–4. (*T. A. Fletcher; John Marshall*)

Plates 15 and 16. Above: 0–6–0 tank No 47487 on a rail-tour train in Riverside station, Liverpool, on 13 June 1964. *Below*: The main arched roof of Liverpool Central station, 14 April 1964. (*John Marshall*)

at Standish, north of Wigan, to join the LUR at Whelley Junction, and four years later a southern connection from the LUR back on to the main line at Bamfurlong south of Wigan. By this means the 'Whelley Loop' was completed by which Wigan could be by-passed.

The Standish line crossed the Douglas Valley on a viaduct of thirteen arches and six iron spans. Through the grounds of Haigh Hall, at the request of the Earl of Crawford & Balcarres, a cut-and-cover tunnel 374yd (342m) long hid the railway from view. It was removed in 1883–4 because of subsidence.

The 'loop' was much used by through freight traffic and by occasional passenger trains, particularly excursions. (See Plate 22.) Connections with the LYR near Hindley and the GCR at Amberswood gave facilities for some interesting through workings. Perhaps the most interesting were the banana trains from Garston. Elders Fyffes transferred to Garston from Manchester in 1912 and by 1936 was despatching over 100,000 tons of bananas annually, mostly by rail. The whole of Scotland's bananas travelled via St Helens and Whelley to join the main line at Standish. Trains were hauled by a variety of locomotives, even LNWR Claughtons and Princes.

Other through workings were Manchester–Blackpool trains via Tyldesley. Near Hindley they joined the former GCR Wigan line (to be mentioned later), shortly turning off again to join the 'Whelley loop' at Amberswood East Junction. From 1911 to 1917, 1922 to 1934, and 1937 to 1964 the Manchester – Windermere 'residential' train ran via this route, or via the LYR and on to the LUR at De Trafford Junction.

When the LYR built its main line from Pendleton, Salford, to Hindley, a connection was made to the Hindley–Blackrod line, enabling traffic between Manchester and Preston to avoid Bolton; this route was used by expresses between Manchester and Blackpool, Edinburgh and Glasgow. There were no heavy engineering works on these lines.

With the opening of the Horwich locomotive works in 1884, a spur was built on to the Horwich branch facing Bolton, enabling trains to run direct from Horwich to Bolton and

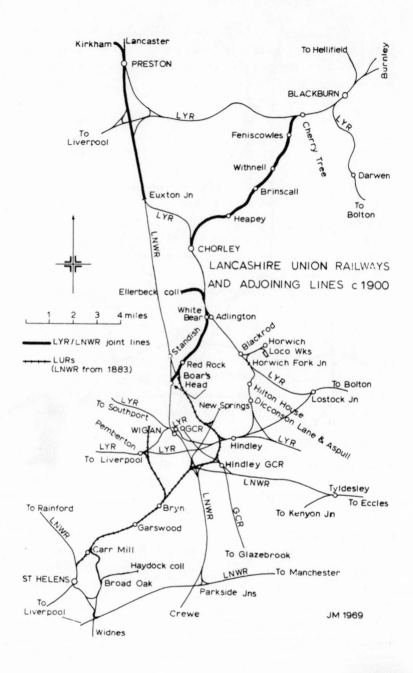

LANCASHIRE UNION RAILWAYS AND ADJOINING LINES c 1900

LYR/LNWR joint lines
LURs (LNWR from 1883)

1 2 3 4 miles

Kirkham Lancaster
PRESTON
To Liverpool
LYR
To Hellifield
Burnley
BLACKBURN
LYR
Feniscowles
Cherry Tree
Withnell
Darwen
Brinscall
To Bolton
Euxton Jn
Heapey
LYR
LNWR
CHORLEY
Ellerbeck coll
White Bear Adlington
Standish
Blackrod
Horwich Loco Wks
Horwich Fork Jn
LYR
Red Rock
Boar's Head
Hilton House
To Bolton
Diceonson Lane & Aspull
Lostock Jn
LYR
To Southport
New Springs
LYR
LYR
WIGAN
GCR
Hindley
LYR
Pemberton
LYR
To Liverpool
Hindley GCR
LNWR
Tyldesley
To Eccles
To Rainford
Bryn
LNWR
GCR
To Kenyon Jn
LNWR
Garswood
Carr Mill
To Glazebrook
Haydock coll
ST HELENS
Broad Oak
LNWR To Manchester
To Liverpool
Parkside Jns
Crewe
Widnes

JM 1969

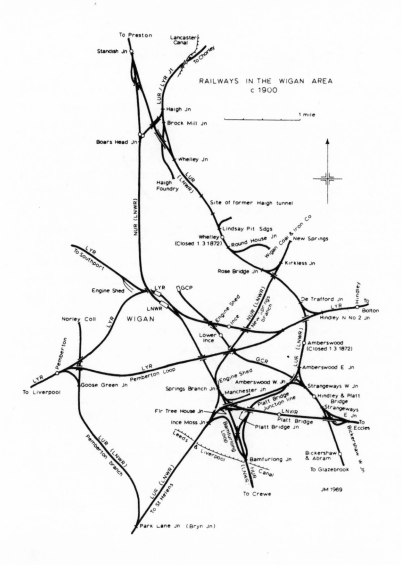

RAILWAYS IN THE WIGAN AREA
c 1900

1 mile

To Preston

Lancaster Canal

Standish Jn

To Chorley

LUR/LYR Jn

Haigh Jn

Brock Mill Jn

Boars Head Jn

Whelley Jn

LUR (LNWR)

Haigh Foundry

Site of former Haigh tunnel

Lindsay Pit Sdgs

Whelley (Closed 1 3 1872)

Round House Jn

Wigan Coal & Iron Co

New Springs

NUR (LNWR)

Rose Bridge Jn

Kirkless Jn

LYR To Southport

Engine Shed

LYR

GCP

LNWR

WIGAN

De Trafford Jn

Hindley

To Bolton

LYR

Hindley N No 2 Jn

Norley Coll

LYR

Ince

Engine Shed

NUR (LNWR)

New Springs branch

Pemberton

Lower Ince

Amberswood (Closed 1 3 1872)

LYR

Pemberton Loop

GCR

Amberswood E Jn

LUR (LNWR)

To Liverpool

Goose Green Jn

Engine Shed

Springs Branch Jn

Amberswood W. Jn

Manchester Jn

Strangeways W Jn

Fir Tree House Jn

Platt Bridge Junction line

Hindley & Platt Bridge

LNWR

Strangeways E Jn

To Eccles

Ince Moss Jn

Bamfurlong Loop

Platt Bridge

Platt Bridge Jn

Bickershaw W Jn

LUR (LNWR) Pemberton branch

Leeds & Liverpool Canal

LUR (LNWR)

Bamfurlong Jn

Bickershaw & Abram

To Glazebrook

JM 1969

To St Helens

To Crewe

Park Lane Jn (Bryn Jn)

Manchester. The 'Horwich Fork' opened in 1887. Through passenger trains were advertised as running 'via Fork'.

As coal production in the Wigan area came to an end traffic over the lines declined. Latterly the passenger services were little used and the Blackburn–Chorley–Wigan trains via Boar's

Head and Hindley were withdrawn in January 1960. Freight traffic continued for a few more years until it could be disposed of or re-routed.

From the early 1900s the Bolton Corporation trams and later buses took most of the Horwich traffic. Latterly the passenger traffic was largely locomotive works employees on privilege tickets. The afternoon departure for Blackrod was so little used that it was left in a siding because it was not worth the bother of putting it in the platform behind the Bolton train. The author and his two sons made return trips to Horwich from Lostock Junction in May and September 1965 and received consecutively numbered tickets. So the branch was closed, and the 'fork' is now submerged beneath the M61 motorway. Lostock Junction station was closed shortly afterwards.

The Whelley loop was heavily used during electrification of the main line through Wigan and rebuilding of Wigan station, but when this was completed the increased main line capacity made the loop redundant and it was abandoned. All that now remains of this system of lines is the Wigan–St Helens section used by diesel multiple-units to and from Liverpool.

Although the Botany Brow and Boar's Head viaducts have been demolished, there is much of interest still to be seen, and long sections are walkable.

Ormskirk–Rainford–St Helens

The Liverpool & Manchester Railway Act of 1845 contained two attempts to baulk the construction of the Liverpool & Bury Railway. One, already described in Chapter 2, was the Patricroft–Clifton branch. The other was a branch from the St Helens Railway to Rainford, but this was not built and in 1848 the LYR opened the Liverpool & Bury line which passed just north of Rainford.

The opening-up of a coalfield in the Skelmersdale area resulted in the Liverpool, Ormskirk & Preston company obtaining authority in its Act of 1846 for a branch from Ormskirk to Skelmersdale. No progress was made with this until the ELR, as successor to the LO&P, obtained an Act in 1853 to extend the branch to Rainford.

This aroused the St Helens Railway & Canal Co which, also in 1853, obtained powers to build a line from St Helens to Rainford. Both lines were opened in 1858 and by means of a bridge over the LYR formed a through route from Ormskirk to St Helens, with spurs to join the LYR at Rainford Junction. (See map, page 79.) Both sections were double track.

A passenger service was operated between Ormskirk and Rainford Junction by the ELR, and between there and St Helens by the St Helens Railway. In 1859 the ELR was amalgamated with the LYR. In 1864 the LNWR absorbed the St Helens Railway and in the same Act granted running powers to the LYR between Rainford Junction and St Helens.

In 1906 the LYR introduced railmotors between Ormskirk and Rainford Junction and opened three ground-level halts. A service of nineteen return trips operated on weekdays and eleven on Sundays, taking 18 min for the 6 mile (9.7km) journey. On the LNWR portion there were eight trains on weekdays, none on Saturdays and three on Sundays, taking 20 minutes for the 5½ miles (8.9km). The railmotors later worked through to St Helens, but always calling at Rainford Junction, and another halt was opened on the St Helens section. This portion served no centres of population apart from Rainford village, but passenger services survived World War II until 1951. The poorly-used trains on the Skelmersdale branch ran until 1956. Freight traffic continued until the early 1960s. Both sections were dismantled soon after closure, just as work was beginning on Skelmersdale new town.

Glazebrook to Wigan Central and St Helens

The rich coalfield between West Leigh and Wigan naturally interested many railway promoters, and in 1873 the Wigan

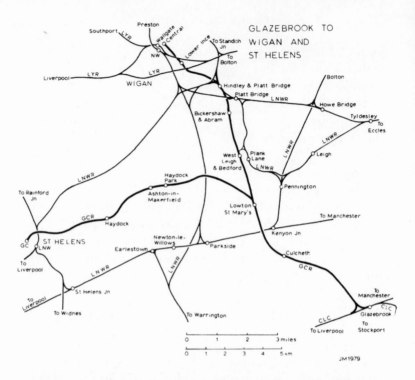

Junction Railways Company was formed to build a line connecting it to the Cheshire Railway at Glazebrook. The GNR refused to support it, so it went ahead with the backing of the MS&L and Midland companies, and obtained an Act in 1874. Later the Midland withdrew, so it was with MS&L support guided by Edward Watkin that the line was built.

It was opened for coal traffic in 1879, with double track, to a temporary terminus at Strangeways near Hindley. Passenger trains began in 1884 when the line was extended into Wigan. A new station in Wigan was opened in 1892 when the first station was closed. (See Plate 23.) From Glazebrook to Wigan Central was a distance of 11¾ miles (19km).

Apart from some substantial underbridges in blue bricks and wrought-iron at Wigan there was little significant engineering. Trains were worked from the start by the MS&L (GCR from 1897), running through to Manchester Central. Besides connections to several collieries there were two connections

94

from Strangeways to the Lancashire Union line at Amberswood East and West Junctions, opened in 1880. The opening of the connection from Strangeways East Junction to Bickershaw Junction on the LNWR Tyldesley–Wigan line in 1886 opened up a new route for LNWR trains from Manchester on to the Whelley Loop to join the LNWR main line at Standish, so avoiding Wigan. The use of this route has already been mentioned.

Several expresses ran non-stop between Manchester Central and Glazebrook, reaching Wigan, 21¼ miles (34km) in 45 min. This compared favourably with the LYR time of 48 min for the 18 miles (29km) via Bolton, but was poor compared with the LNWR time of 33–37 min for expresses over about the same distance. With the opening of the new route via Walkden the LYR was able to offer a non-stop time of 24 min. At Glazebrook the WJR offered connections to Stockport via the CLC.

The branch from the WJR at Lowton St Mary's to St Helens was again promoted locally by the St Helens & Wigan Junction Railway Company, incorporated by Act of 1885 with powers to enter into traffic arrangements with the WJR and the MS&L, and five years to complete the line. The creeping pace of construction did little to lessen the ambition of the company which, in 1889, changed its name to the Liverpool, St Helens & South Lancashire Railway with a view to extending to Liverpool, but this extension was never authorised. Goods traffic began in 1895.

Double track extended from Lowton St Mary's to Ashton in Makerfield from where it was single into St Helens. At length, in 1900, passenger trains began, taking 20 min for the 8¼ miles (13.2km) between Lowton St Mary's and St Helens. Passengers changed at the junction for trains to Manchester. As on the WJR, trains were worked by the GCR.

With astounding audacity, in its timetable the Great Central advertised connections between St Helens and Liverpool and Southport via Glazebrook and the Cheshire Lines, a distance of 38½ miles (62km) to Liverpool taking about 1 hr 20 min compared with the direct LNWR route of 11½ miles (18.5km) taking about 25 min. The journey to Southport, 54 miles (87km), would doubtless appeal to railway enthusiasts as the fare would be the same as via Wigan but the journey time, anything from 1 hr 40 min to 4 hr 5 min, could hardly attract the family out for a day by the sea.

The new line did offer a good service between St Helens and Manchester, 23½ miles (37.8km) in about 55 min which compared favourably with the LNWR 21½ miles (34.6km) via St Helens Junction, and it offered the best service of all between St Helens and Stockport.

On 1 January 1906 both the WJR and the St Helens line were absorbed by the GCR, becoming part of the LNER on 1 January 1923.

Both routes duplicated other lines, and by the 1960s their traffic could easily be transferred. The St Helens line lost its passenger trains in 1952, though special trains continued to serve Haydock Park on meeting days at the local racecourse. The Wigan line became a victim of the Beeching re-shaping programme and by the mid-1960s the lines were largely out of use. Freight traffic continued to Wigan from Bickershaw Junction on the LNWR Tyldesley line until 1967. In 1968 a spur was opened from Golborne Junction on the Warrington – Wigan main line to join the St Helens line at Edge Green. This enabled the section from Glazebrook to Edge Green through Lowton St Mary's to be closed and tank traffic to the Shell Oil Haydock Terminal to be worked from the main line.

CHAPTER 6

The Lune Valley

Clapham–Ingleton–Low Gill and Wennington–Lancaster–Morecambe

By the mid–1840s the principal English towns were connected by railways to London; promoters were now looking towards Scotland. The Lancaster & Carlisle was under construction, while in Yorkshire the Leeds & Bradford Railway was extending to Skipton and Colne. By building from Skipton to the Lancaster & Carlisle, a route could be established to Scotland from the great manufacturing towns of Yorkshire. With this object the North Western Railway Company was incorporated in 1846 with powers to build a railway from the L&B north-west of Skipton to join the L&C at Low Gill, south of Tebay, and a branch from Clapham to Lancaster, and gave powers to lease the works to the NWR or the L&C. The NWR secured the lease.

By the time construction started costs were rising rapidly, so it was decided to cut the Low Gill line short at Ingleton and to concentrate on the branch to Lancaster and Morecambe. A further NWR Act authorised a connection to the L&C at Lancaster. First to be completed was the single-line Morecambe–Lancaster section, 3 miles (4.8km), in 1848, though it was open for 18 months before the connection to the L&C was ready. In 1849 trains were running to Ingleton from where passengers could reach the L&C at Milnthorpe by a stagecoach service. With completion of the single-line Clapham–Lancaster section in 1850 the Ingleton service was withdrawn and the line was closed· to passengers. Traffic to Morecambe built up over the years until the town became 'Bradford on t'Sea'. Today much of Morecambe's population

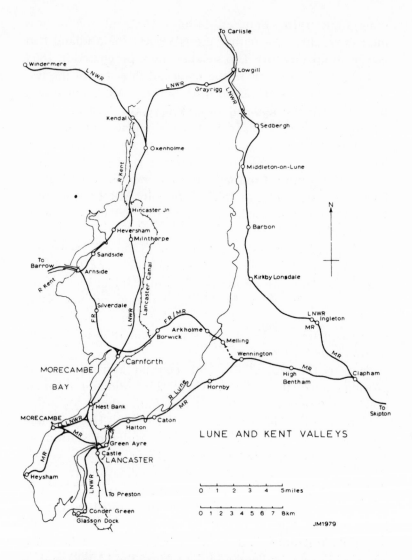

LUNE AND KENT VALLEYS

JM1979

is of Yorkshire origin, thanks to the NWR.

In 1852 the NWR entered into an operating agreement with the Midland, which thus gained control of the traffic northwest of Leeds. By its Act of 1852 the NWR obtained powers to operate steamers between Morecambe and Piel Pier (see Chapter 7) and the Midland agreed to work this service. At the same time traffic between Morecambe and Belfast was increasing, although neither the NWR nor the Midland had powers to operate this. Two steamers were purchased in 1854 and registered privately in the names of directors of the two companies, and were put to work between Morecambe and Belfast. With the lease of the NWR to the Midland from 1 January 1859 the Midland assumed complete control.

In 1865 the Midland replaced the two steamers by a new one named *Roe*, but in 1867 this was transferred to the Barrow Steam Navigation Company to operate from Piel Pier, following the opening in 1867 of the joint MR/FR line from Wennington to Carnforth, which gave the Midland a through route to Piel.

The Midland lost its stronghold at Morecambe in 1864 when the LNWR opened the branch from the Lancaster & Carlisle at Hest Bank. The lease of the NWR to the Midland ended on 1 January 1871 when the Midland purchased the NWR outright. The single-line Lancaster and Morecambe branch from Clapham was doubled in stages from 1850 to 1889, as shown in the Gazetteer.

Towards the end of the 19th century Morecambe was proving inadequate as a port, so in 1892 the Midland obtained powers to open a new port at Heysham, about 3½ miles (5.6km) south of Morecambe. The extension to Heysham was opened on 11 July 1904. The new Midland station at Morecambe Promenade, opened on 24 March 1907, acknowledged the town's now principal role as a holiday resort.

Beyond Ingleton no progress was made until in 1857 the L&C obtained an Act to build the line from Low Gill to Ingleton, 18½ miles (29.8km), to provide a connection with the Midland Railway via the NWR. However, in 1859 the NWR was leased to the Midland and the L&C to the LNWR, so that by the time the double-track line to Ingleton was completed in 1861 it was the LNWR which found itself confronting its bitterest enemy across the deep gorge of the Greta at Ingleton, with a viaduct connecting the two companies' stations. The single-line Clapham–Ingleton section, 4¼ miles (6.8km), was doubled and passenger trains were restored, but passengers were at first compelled to walk between the stations at Ingleton, down to the river and up again. Even then their troubles were not over, for at Low Gill 'connections' between main line and branch were arranged for the maximum inconvenience.

It was this intolerable obstruction by the LNWR which eventually forced the Midland to obtain an Act for the Settle–Carlisle line. This so alarmed the LNWR that it at last made a satisfactory agreement for through traffic. The Midland then tried to abandon its Settle–Carlisle project, but this was prevented by the North British and Glasgow & South Western Railways which sought to gain from it. Its completion in 1876 made the Ingleton route redundant, so traffic over it never developed except when the Settle–Carlisle line was blocked by snow. It is extraordinary that passenger traffic lasted as long as it did, surviving both world wars, until 1954. The line remained open as a through freight route, proving its worth in the winter of January to March 1963 when the Settle–Carlisle line was blocked. The last through freight train ran in 1966 and the line was dismantled shortly afterwards.

The abandonment of the Clapham–Low Gill line was a direct outcome of short-sighted Victorian railway politics, involving expenditure and waste on a vast scale. The cost of the Settle–Carlisle line in 1876 was £3,500,000, equivalent to £152,100,000 in 1991, and considerable loss of life, all of which could have been avoided. It is arguable that a wiser course would have been to electrify from Leeds to Low Gill, to take advantage of the greater line capacity of the electrified railway over Shap, and to abandon the Settle–Carlisle line. The Ingleton line was a grand scenic route. Today it makes a fine long-distance walk. (See Plate 25.)

In 1908 the Lancaster–Morecambe–Heysham line became a testing ground for a high-voltage single-phase ac electrification experiment using current at 6,600V, 25Hz. Rolling stock, built at Derby, comprised three motor coaches and four trailers. Electrical equipment was supplied by Siemens (two) and Dick

Kerr (one). These vehicles ran for over forty years until, practically falling apart, they were withdrawn on 11 February 1951. During a short period of steam operation the line was converted to a 50Hz system, still at 6,600V, and electric operation was resumed on 17 August using suitably rebuilt ex-LNWR stock, itself by then nearly forty years old, having originally been built for the Earl's Court–Willesden line. Further experiments with the overhead equipment were made in 1955–6 in connection with the BR high-voltage ac work.

The Wennington–Lancaster section, 10½ miles (16.9km), gave the passenger a pleasant run along the broad Lune Valley through a quiet agricultural landscape with patches of woodland. Between Caton and Halton the line crossed a loop of the Lune by two girder bridges. At Halton the village, on the opposite side of the Lune, was connected to the station by a wooden bridge. This was washed away in a flood on 8 February 1896 and it was replaced in September by the present iron bridge. Between Halton and Lancaster the line passed through one of the arches of John Rennie's great aqueduct of 1797 carrying the Lancaster Canal over the Lune. At Lancaster, beyond the junction with the single-track spur to Castle station, the line swung across the Lune on an iron girder bridge and at Scale Hall turned away north-westwards to reach Morecambe. (See Plate 24.)

After closure of the Wennington–Lancaster–Morecambe section trains were re-routed between Wennington and Lancaster via the Midland/Furness joint line to Carnforth. Trains to Morecambe from Carnforth or Lancaster use the former LNWR line from Hest Bank.

Lancaster–Glasson Dock

Navigation of the River Lune up to Lancaster was possible only for small vessels, and silting was a constant problem. To enable larger vessels to serve Lancaster a dock was constructed at Glasson on the south side of the estuary, and opened in 1787.

At first, communication with Lancaster was by road, or by smaller boats, until the Glasson branch of the Lancaster Canal was opened in 1826. This allowed small coasting vessels to reach Lancaster, Kendal and Preston. The canal was leased to the LNWR in 1864.

To give speedier access to the dock the LNWR opened a branch railway 5 miles (8km) long from the north end of Lancaster station in 1883. There was one intermediate station, at Conder Green, a mile from Glasson Dock. Passenger traffic was never heavy. Following the opening of Preston Dock in 1892 freight traffic declined but the line remained open, losing its passenger trains in the depression of 1930, and freight trains in 1964.

CHAPTER 7

Cumbria, South

The railways of western Cumbria owe their development almost entirely to the rich deposits of haematite iron-ore in the north and south of the region and to the collieries around Whitehaven. While the mines prospered so did the railways; exhaustion of the iron-ore greatly reduced traffic and several railways had to close. Today the southern, western and northern fringes of the Lake District are strewn with abandoned railways originally belonging to nearly a dozen different companies, whose complex histories can only be sketched here, but some lines provide interesting walks.

Furness Railway: Arnside–Hincaster

Coke was needed for smelting the iron, and as the Cumbrian coal was not the best for producing coke most of it came from County Durham via the North Eastern (former Stockton & Darlington) Railway over Stainmore to Kirkby Stephen. From there trains for northern Cumbria used the 1862 line towards Penrith, and those for south Cumbria the 1861 line to Tebay, from where they travelled south along the LNWR to Carnforth. Here they reversed to travel over the Furness Railway.

To cut out this reversal, in 1867 the Furness Railway obtained powers for a 5 ¼ mile (8.5km) line from Arnside to a junction with the LNWR at Hincaster, almost at the point where it crossed the tunnel on the Lancaster Canal. The Act ruled that in order to cause minimum obstruction to the view from Dallam Tower Estate the railway was to be carried on 'arches and pillars' where it crossed the River Beela beside the Kent estuary. An attractive viaduct was built here with three main cast-iron arch spans and approach spans of stone arches. The single-track line was built by James Nelson, contractor. There were two intermediate stations, at Sandside and Heversham. (See map, page 98.)

The line was opened in 1876, but curiously coke traffic continued via Carnforth until 1914 when, as a result of pressure during World War I, it began to travel via Sandside. In 1876 the FR put on a weekday service of five passenger trains each way between Grange-over-Sands and Kendal, using running powers over the LNWR. It was a pleasant journey, over the Kent viaduct and along beside the estuary, to Hincaster, Oxenholme, and down the branch to Kendal, with views of hills all the way. FR locomotives would work through to Kendal. In summer the Windermere portion of through Leeds–Lakeside trains via the Midland/Furness joint line would be detached at Arnside for the run to Windermere via Hincaster. An interesting service was operated by the North Eastern Railway via Kirkby Stephen for the benefit of Durham miners, who had a convalescent home at Conishead Priory, south of Ulverston. For a while the LNER worked this service with a Sentinel steam railcar.

The local passenger traffic ended in 1942. Coke traffic continued until 1963 for Millom ironworks. After that the line became simply a siding from Arnside to the quarry at Sandside until this traffic ended in 1972.

Conishead Priory branch

The operational difficulties of the Ulverston–Barrow line, with its curves and gradients to the summit at Lindal, were such that at the height of its prosperity the Furness Railway considered a route nearer the coast, the line through Lindal and Dalton being left to serve the mines. Following the opening of the North Lonsdale Company's ironworks just south of the

Plates 17 and 18. *Above*: Train entering James Street station, Liverpool Overhead Railway. (*W. A. Camwell*). *Below*: The only remaining monument to the Liverpool Overhead Railway: the entrance to Dingle tunnel, above Herculaneum Dock, on 3 May 1970. The inscription above reads L.O.R.ᵞ/1896 Southern Extension 1896./Engineers Sir Douglas Fox J. H. Greathead E. R. Cotterell/H. M. Nowell C. Braddock Contractors/Sir William Forwood Chairman. (*John Marshall*)

Plates 19 and 20. *Above*: Hadlow Road station on the former GWR/LNWR joint Hooton–West Kirby line, restored as a country station museum, 1 September 1979. *Below*: LNER D9 class 4–4–0 No 2306 (former GCR No 1015) on the 17.20 to Warrington at Southport Lord Street, 29 April 1948. (*John Marshall, W. A. Camwell*)

Ulverston Canal in 1874 powers were obtained for a branch of about 2½ miles (4km) from Plumpton Junction east of Ulverston, crossing the Ulverston Canal by an opening bridge, and terminating at Conishead Priory near Bardsea.

It was 1883 before the branch was ready; by then the brief period of prosperity had ended and there was no further extension. Two trains a day each way from Ulverston, reversing at the junction and taking 12 min on the run, gave the passenger a choice of 36 min or 4 hr 41 min at Conishead Hydro. By the turn of the century the train service had been reduced to one per day giving only 6 min at Conishead. Surprisingly, this lasted until the end of 1916.

Like most FR stations, Conishead Priory station was an attractive building, but its situation, almost enclosed in dense woodland and remote from any centre of population, was unlikely to attract traffic, particularly for a stay of six minutes. After closure the northern portion of the branch continued to serve the ironworks and later the Glaxo laboratories.

Piel Pier branch, Barrow

The author still retains vivid memories of being fascinated as a child by a woodcut in a copy of the 1878 edition of Williams' *Midland Railway* inherited from his grandfather, showing a bird's-eye view of Piel pier, tremendously long and with trains running along it to the steamer station at the end. In the distance was Roa Island and the embankment connecting it to Rampside, near Barrow.

The history of the pier goes back before the incorporation of the Furness Railway, which was originally planned to connect the iron mines at Lindal and slate quarries at Kirkby with a shipping berth at Barrow. In 1840 John Abel Smith, a prominent London builder with large interests in the Preston & Wyre Railway and the town of Fleetwood, bought Roa Island, measuring about 300 x 200yd (274 x 183m), near Rampside for £500, with the intention of building an embankment to

Woodcut of Piel Pier, from Williams' *Midland Railway* 1878

connect it 'with the neighbouring island of Great Britain'; and also a pier out to Piel Island. A Bill for a pier was promoted by Sir Peter Hesketh Fleetwood in 1841, but it failed. A revised Bill for a pier turning westwards into deep water in the Piel Channel succeeded in 1843, authorising Smith to construct the pier and embankment at his own expense.

The Furness Railway was now forced to build a branch to Rampside because Smith would otherwise have built a competing line, and it was included in the Furness Railway Act of incorporation in 1844. The railway company entered into an agreement with Smith whereby it would extend the railway along the embankment and on to the pier if Smith would complete the pier, but there was nothing in the agreement about opening the pier for traffic. Although Smith undertook to have the pier ready for the opening of the railway in 1846 it was not completed, so from 3 June the FR worked slate and iron-ore trains to a jetty at Barrow.

The Piel branch left the main line at Roose. There was a station at Rampside followed by a wooden trestle of sixteen

12ft (3.66m) spans and an embankment 3,000ft (914m) long. At Roa Island it turned sharply west and on to the pier. This was a timber trestle on three levels. The first and highest, 810ft (247m) long, carried the rails and was used for slate and iron traffic at high water. The next level, 6ft 6in (2m) lower was 370ft (113m) long and the third was a low-water pier 100ft (30m) long. Another pier 200ft (61m) long branched southwards from the main pier, 40ft (12.2m) above low water.

A month before the passenger service began the wind reached such a force that a trolley with a sail travelled along the embankment at 30mph (48km/h). Several people enjoyed this preliminary ride.

As Smith's steamer was still not ready on the opening date for passengers, 24 August 1846, an emergency service was run by the wooden paddle steamer *Ayrshire Lassie*, 'weather permitting', leaving Fleetwood at 11.00 and 14.00 and Piel at 13.00 and 16.00, taking 45 minutes, connecting with trains to and from Preston.

It was withdrawn after two months beacuse the single-line FR could not handle both passenger and freight traffic. Doubling between Roose and Millwood junctions was put in hand in 1847. An unsatisfactory agreement was reached between Smith and the FR, but at the date for the resumption of passenger traffic Smith's steamer still was not ready, so in March 1847 the FR bought the small steamer *Windermere*, which had been operating between Liverpool and Ulverston from 1834, renovated it, renamed it *Helvellyn* and advertised a service between Piel and Fleetwood to begin on 24 May 1847. Smith insisted on conditions for landing passengers at the pier which were unacceptable to the FR, so the sailings were transferred to Barrow to start on 1 June. The timetable had to be varied according to the tides and the service was not popular.

In May 1848 agreement was reached and *Helvellyn* began operating on a fixed schedule between Fleetwood and Piel Pier until the end of the summer. During the following winter the Piel branch was closed because it was not covering expenses. Smith wanted to sell his works to the FR and in 1851 tried to force the issue by promoting a Bill for a line of his own to Lindal. This was successfully blocked by the FR, and the Bill was withdrawn. Negotiations were now opened between Smith and the FR and at length terms were agreed upon which the FR would lease the embankment, Roa Island and pier for 999 years. Before this could be confirmed a severe storm on 27 December 1852 destroyed a third of the pier and a wooden goods shed on Roa Island and damaged the embankment. Smith tried to hold the FR to the terms of the agreement but failed and in the end he was glad to dispose of the entire works for £15,000. Repairs to the pier and embankment cost the FR £1,645.

Following the opening of the Ulverstone (*sic*) & Lancaster Railway in 1857, providing a link to the Lancaster & Carlisle Railway at Carnforth, the Fleetwood service was reduced to summers-only. The L&C was leased to the LNWR in 1859 and the U&L was absorbed by the FR in 1862.

In 1867 the Furness & Midland joint line was opened from Carnforth to Wennington on the former North Western line from Skipton to Lancaster. To accommodate the Midland trains the FR rebuilt Piel pier with a station at the end. On 1 July 1867 the steamer *Herald* began a service to Douglas, Isle of Man, operated by the Barrow Steam Navigation Co, owned jointly by the FR, Midland and James Little & Co, to connect with the 1000 train from Leeds to Piel. The BSN then purchased three small paddle steamers which had worked between Morecambe and Belfast, and on 1 September 1867 inaugurated a service to Belfast. The Midland ran through coaches from Leeds to Piel connecting with the 1130 Midland express from King's Cross (St Pancras was not opened until the following year). Throughout this period *Helvellyn* maintained a service between Piel and Fleetwood until replaced in 1867 by *Walney*. So began the glorious decade of Piel Pier, from which period would date the woodcut in Williams' *Midland Railway*, reproduced on page 108.

In 1878 the Ramsden dock at Barrow was completed, and in 1881 the FR opened a station adjacent to it. From 1 June 1881 the Isle of Man steamers were transferred to the new dock and the Belfast service followed in October. Piel pier was closed and the connection from Roose Junction to Parrock Hall Junction was abandoned on 27 March 1882.

A new station was built on Roa Island, still named Piel, and to this windy and desolate spot the FR ran a service of seven trains each way to and from Barrow. Piel pier was left to rot until 1891 when it was dismantled. The most amazing fact in the whole history of the Piel branch is that the train service survived until 6 July 1936.

Coniston Branch

The original Furness Railway opened in 1846 included a line to Kirkby in Furness, leaving the main line at Millwood Junction just north of Furness Abbey. At about the same time as its opening further powers were obtained to extend it to Broughton-in-Furness to provide an outlet for copper ore from around Coniston. This extension was opened in 1848. In 1850 it was joined at Foxfield by the Whitehaven & Furness Junction Railway and the section from Foxfield to Broughton then became a branch.

The difficulties of transporting the ore to Broughton led to the Coniston Railway Act of 1857 authorising a railway from Broughton to the mines above Coniston. It was opened in 1859 and was worked by the FR, in which it was vested in 1862. From its opening the single line was worked as a branch from Foxfield.

Besides providing an outlet for the mineral traffic it was an attractive tourist line to a part of the Lake District which had been difficult to reach. The branch passed through delightful scenery all the way. There were stations at Woodland and Torver, and at Coniston, at a considerable height above the town, a handsome station with an overall roof. (See Plate 26.) Beyond the station the branch continued to the mines. The total length from Foxfield was about 10 miles (16km).

Starting almost from sea level at Foxfield the line climbed from Broughton, beginning at 1 in 49, to reach a height of 345ft (105m), the highest point on the FR, between Woodland and Torver. Beyond Torver there were attractive views over Coniston Water.

To provide trips on the lake in connection with the trains the Coniston Railway obtained a most extraordinary steamboat. It was built by Jones, Quiggin & Co of Liverpool in 1859 and named *Gondola*, presumably because a Venetian gondola was about the only thing with which it could be compared. It measured 84ft (25.6m) long, 14ft 2in (4.318m) wide and had a draught of 4ft 6in (1.372m) at the stern and only 1ft 0in (0.3048m) at the bow. Its cabin, furnished like something out of the Great Exhibition of 1851, accommodated 225 passengers. At the stern was a locomotive-type boiler and a two-cylinder simple engine driving a 4ft 0in (1.219m) diameter four-blade bronze propeller. She worked on the lake until 1940, was disposed of in 1944, and became a houseboat. In 1964 she was sunk to preserve the hull. In 1977 the hull was recovered and the vessel was rebuilt at Coniston Hall under the auspices of the National Trust, the new owners. *Gondola* was magnificently restored and returned to public service on Coniston Water in July 1980. In 1908 *Gondola's* services were supplemented by a new turbine ship *Lady of the Lake* which ran until 1950.

Another interesting feature of the branch was its working for a period by one of the two FR steam railmotors built in 1905. It ran with a four-wheeled trailer coach. They were withdrawn in 1918.

During LMS and BR days the passenger service was operated by a pull-and-push set. There were eight trains daily, and one between Foxfield and Broughton, which were well used by the local people and in summer by long-distance travellers. In addition there were summer excursions from Blackpool and Morecambe twice weekly.

In 1958 BR claimed that passenger traffic on the branch involved annual losses of over £16,000 and proposed to withdraw the service. Protests and explanations were useless; there was a strong suspicion that the accounts had been falsified, and in October the passenger trains were withdrawn without any effort to economise in operating costs. Staffing, signalling and maintenance were all excessive. Following closure the losses on alternative bus services, road improvements and loss of trade were as much as it would have cost to operate a light diesel service, with various other economies. Closure caused widespread inconvenience and bitterness. The thrice-weekly goods train ran until April 1962, usually hauled by a 3F 0–6–0 tank from Barrow shed.

The Whitehaven, Cleator & Egremont Railway

The WCE, like the other lines in west Cumbria, was built to carry iron-ore. Its main line ran from a junction with the Whitehaven & Furness Junction Railway at Mirehouse Junction about 2 miles (3.2km) south of Whitehaven, through Cleator Moor and Rowrah to the LNWR Cockermouth & Workington line at Marron Junction, 16 miles (25.7km). From Moor Row near Cleator Moor a branch turned southwards through Egremont to join the Whitehaven & Furness Junction Railway at Sellafield, 7 miles (11.2km). From Ullock Junction on the Rowrah–Marron Junction section the Gilgarron branch ran westward to Parton on the LNWR (Whitehaven Junction) just north of Whitehaven, 7½ miles (12km).

The first sections to be authorised, in 1854, were from Mirehouse Junction to Egremont and the 'branch' from Moor Row to Frizington, opened in January 1857 for mineral traffic. With an outlet to the sea at Whitehaven, the iron-ore mines at Egremont, Cleator and Frizington developed rapidly and soon the railway was carrying heavy traffic. Fortunately, the gradients favoured the loads. In July 1857 passenger trains began running, serving stations at Moor Row, Woodend and Egremont, Cleator Moor and Frizington. So successful was the railway that in 1861 an extension was authorised from

To Carlisle
Bullgill
M & C
MARYPORT
Dearham Bridge
M & C
Dearham
Flimby
Linefoot
LNWR
Papcastle
Great Broughton
Siddick
C & WJ
Brigham
C & W
COCKERMOUTH
CK & P
Seaton
LNWR
Camerton
Marron Jn
Broughton Cross
To Penrith
Workington Bridge
WORKINGTON
Bridgefoot
Main
Central
C & W
WC & E
Harrington Jn
Harrington
Branthwaite
Rose Hill
Distington
Ullock Jn
Lowca Lt
WC & E
WC & E
Lowca
WC & E
Oatlands
Lamplugh
Parton
C & WJ
C & WJ
Bransty
Moresby Parks
WHITEHAVEN
Arlecdon
Rowrah
Kelton Fell
Corkickle
Winder
Mowbray
Yeathouse
FR
Keekle viaduct
Birks Br Jn
N
Mirehouse Jn
WC & E
Eskett
WC & E
Frizington
CLEATOR MOOR
Moor Row
FR
Woodend
WC & E
St. Bees
Gillfoot
EGREMONT

RAILWAYS OF
NORTH-WEST CUMBRIA

Beckermet iron mine

0   1   2   3 miles
0   1   2   3   4   5 km

Nethertpwn
Cleator & Furness
Beckermet
Braystones

C & W   Cockermouth & Workington
C & WJ   Cleator & Workington Junction
CK & P   Cockermouth Keswick & Penrith
FR   Furness
Lowca Lt   Harrington & Lowca Light
WC & E   Whitehaven Cleator & Egremont

Sellafield
To Barrow

JM 1979

Frizington to Lamplugh to serve further iron-ore mines. In 1863 another Act authorised an extension down the Marron valley to a 'Y' junction with the Cockermouth & Workington Railway, so giving an outlet to Workington. The same Act authorised a northern 'loop' at Cleator Moor, opened in 1866.

Mineral trains began running from Lamplugh to Whitehaven in 1862 and northwards to Marron Junction in 1866. Passenger services were extended to Rowrah in 1864 serving stations at Yeathouse and Winder, and in 1866 ran through to Marron Junction, with stops at Wright Green, Ullock, Branthwaite and Bridgefoot. Following closure of Marron Junction station in 1897 trains ran to and from Workington. Wright Green was renamed Lamplugh in 1901.

South of Egremont there were further iron-ore deposits at Beckermet, in which the Whitehaven & Furness Junction Railway had been interested. Agreement was reached in a joint WCE and WFJ Bill in 1865 which became the Cleator & Furness Act of 1866, authorising the extension from Egremont via Beckermet to join the WFJ at Sellafield. In the same session of 1866 the WFJ was amalgamated with the Furness. The new line was opened in 1869 and a passenger service was run between Moor Row and Sellafield.

One other section remains to be described: the Gilgarron branch from Ullock to Distington and Parton. The portion from Ullock Junction to Distington was authorised in 1875 and was opened in 1879, serving an ironworks and a colliery. From Distington where it joined the Cleator & Workington Junction Railway, an extension was authorised in 1876 to join the LNWR, former Whitehaven Junction, at Parton. This portion was opened in 1881.

It was mainly a mineral line, but it did carry a passenger service for two short periods. From 1881–3 there were two trains a day between Whitehaven and Distington, and the service was restored from 1913 to 1914. The Ullock–Parton line was the first section of the WCE to be abandoned. Distington ironworks closed in 1922 and a few years later Wythemoor Colliery became worked out and the line went out of use down to about 1½ miles (2.4km) from Parton where it was joined by a branch to Lowca Colliery. This remained in use until May 1973.

For many years the WCE resisted approaches by the LNWR for amalgamation, but traffic was good enough to enable it to prosper without help from its mighty neighbour. However, with the threat of the Cleator & Workington Junction Railway, being projected in 1876–7, the WCE finally accepted amalgamation with the LNWR, confirmed by an Act of 1877. Following strong protests by the FR, a further Act in 1878 amalgamated the WCE jointly with the FR and LNWR. Joint operation began in February 1880.

All the WCE lines were single-track as built, but many sections were doubled later. They were all steeply-graded, in bleak, sparsely-populated upland country, and passenger trains, weekdays only, were slow and infrequent. The 7½ miles (12km) from Moor Row to Sellafield took 21 min. Services varied: in 1910 there were five each way, with extra trains between Egremont and Moor Row. The 17¼ miles (27.7km) from Whitehaven via Cleator Moor and Rowrah to Bridgefoot took 54 min. From here two trains ran to Cockermouth, 22 miles (35.4km) taking another 20 min, and two to Workington, 22¼ miles (35.8km), taking a further 16 min. Passenger services between Moor Row and Marron Junction were withdrawn by the LMS during the depression of 1931, but the Whitehaven–Moor Row–Egremont–Sellafield service continued until 1935. For a few years from 1939 the sections from Moor Row to Rowrah, Cleator Moor to Birks Bridge Junction, and the old iron-ore sidings at Frizington were used for storage of surplus coaches. The LMS restored passenger trains between Sellafield and Whitehaven via Egremont in 1946, but they were withdrawn in 1947. After that there were a few excursions, and workmen's trains between Egremont and Sellafield to serve the Calder Hall 'power station'. Plate 27 illustrates one of these. The route was closed to regular freight traffic in 1964 but the track was retained from Mirehouse Junction through Moor Row and Egremont to the Beckermet iron mine. This was served until October 1980 by one or two daily trains of mineral wagons, hauled by a class 25 diesel locomotive.

Cleator Moor on the original 1857 line remained in use for freight until 1972. The last train from Moor Row to Rowrah Quarry ran in February 1978. The track was lifted in 1980.

The Cleator & Workington Junction Railway

The LNWR and the WCE, believing themselves secure with their monopoly of the west Cumberland iron-ore traffic, pushed up their charges until by the mid 1870s it was reported that in west Cumberland haulage of iron-ore was costing much more than the same traffic over the same distance in South Wales. The leading ironmasters of west Cumberland were not men to be bullied by Euston, and in 1875 Lords Lonsdale and Leconfield and Henry Frazer of Curwen of Workington promoted a Bill for a railway from a junction with the WCE at Cleator Moor to a junction with the LNWR Whitehaven Junction Railway at Siddick north of Workington, with branches at Harrington and Workington.

Despite expected opposition from the LNWR, the Bill succeeded and the Cleator & Workington Junction Railway Company was incorporated in 1876. Under an agreement of 6 April 1877, confirmed by an Act the following June, the Furness Railway undertook to work the C&WJ from its opening for a third of the receipts. The double-track main line from Cleator to Workington was opened in October 1879 with stations at Cleator Moor, Moresby Parks, Distington, High Harrington and Workington Central. The passenger service was extended to Siddick on the Whitehaven Junction line in 1880. As on the other west Cumbria lines, the passenger service was slow and infrequent. The four trains each way, weekdays only, took around half-an-hour to cover the 12 miles from Moor Row, where they connected with the WCE service to Sellafield, but in view of the hilly route this was a fair performance. The main traffic was minerals and the line soon became busy. In 1911 the railway carried a total of 200,000 passengers and about two million tons of freight. Most of the mineral traffic, as on other railways, was carried in wagons privately owned by the various collieries and ironworks, the trains forming colourful assemblages such as can now be seen only at model railway exhibitions. The use of privately owned mineral wagons ended at the beginning of World War II.

A second C&WJ Act in 1878 authorised a branch from Distington to connect at Rowrah with the Rowrah & Kelton Fell Mineral Railway which had opened in 1877. One of the first directors of the R&KF, R. A. Robinson, was also one of the first of the C&WJ. The R&KF was built by William Baird & Co, Scottish ironmasters, and the single-line C&WJ branch became known as 'Baird's Line'. Mineral traffic began in May 1882. The following year passenger trains began running between Distington and Oatlands on Saturdays. The service was extended to Arlecdon near Rowrah from October 1912 to 1917. Between Distington and Oatlands the passenger service finally ended in 1922 after two earlier periods of closure.

Besides its regular passenger service, the Sellafield–Siddick route was occasionally used as a diversion, although this involved reversal at Moor Row. It was also used for excursions after withdrawal of the regular passenger trains in 1931.

The main line climbed from 250ft (76m) at Cleator Moor to 460ft (140m) at Moresby Parks on gradients of 1 in 72 for nearly a mile, and 1 in 70 for 1½ miles (2.4km), then dropped to Distington on similar gradients. At Keekle, about ¾ mile (1km) north of Cleator Moor station, the River Keekle was crossed on a stone viaduct of seven arches. (See Plate 28.) There were several big cuttings and high embankments, and some sharp curves.

The Rowrah branch had the heaviest earthworks and gradients. From its junction with the R&KFM it climbed to cross over the WCE by a girder bridge of 48ft (14.63m) span. Beyond Arlecdon it dropped at 1 in 46 for nearly a mile to a high curving embankment known as Brownrigg Curve, with a radius of 14 chains (282m), across the Dubb Beck Valley, climbing again up the other side at 1 in 60 for 1½ miles to the summit of the entire C&WJ system at about 600ft (182m) in a rock cutting. From here it fell at 1 in 52 for about a mile to Oatlands, where a branch trailed in from a colliery. After a short climb through a rock cutting and a tunnel under a road it plunged down at 1 in 44 for just over 2 miles (3.2km) on sharp reverse curves ending with a drop at 1 in 70 on a 15 chain (302m) curve to a bridge over the C&WJ main line and a 10 chain (201m) curve down to the junction at Distington.

Rowrah & Kelton Fell Mineral Railway

It is convenient to deal with this short line here because of its close connection with the C&WJ. Deposits of haematite ore were known in the Kelton Fell area for many years, and William Baird & Co were interested in it. The WCE had extended through Rowrah in 1862, but high rates at first discouraged the construction of a connecting line.

At length an Act in 1874 authorised the Rowrah & Kelton Fell Mineral Railway, 3½ miles (5.6km) long to join the WCE at Rowrah. It was opened in January 1877 and was worked by William Baird & Co. Gradients were severe for it had to climb from about 580ft (177m) at Rowrah to nearly 900ft (274m) at the Kelton Fell mines. This favoured loaded trains, but haulage of empties was hard work.

The C&WJ branch from Distington crossed over the WCE just west of Rowrah station to join the R&KF line near its junction with the WCE. Offering better rates, the C&WJ was soon taking all the traffic, and with the opening of the Linefoot branch (mentioned below) in 1887 it was able to provide a route via the Maryport & Carlisle and Solway Junction railways into Scotland.

Prosperity was brief and by 1900 the mines were nearly exhausted. Limestone traffic continued, but Baird & Co was no longer interested and tried to dispose of the line. In 1920 it was at last sold for £750 to the Whitehaven Haematite Iron Co of Cleator Moor and the Salter Quarry Co. By 1927 traffic had dwindled almost to nothing and the railway became disused until it was dismantled in 1934.

To continue the C&WJ story, the connection at Siddick with the LNWR involved dealings with that company which the C&WJ wished to avoid, so in 1883 powers were obtained for a line from Calva Junction about a mile north of Workington Central to a junction with the Solway Junction Railway near Aspatria. The same Act also authorised a connection at Cloffocks near Workington from the C&WJ to join the Cockermouth & Workington line (next chapter), and branches to Harrington Harbour and Derwent Ironworks.

While the connection to the Solway Junction Railway was under construction, an Act of 1886 authorised the abandonment of much of it and it was cut short to join the Bullgill–Brigham branch of the Maryport & Carlisle Railway at Linefoot.

Mineral traffic began in 1887, and in 1888 passenger trains began running between Workington and Seaton, 2½ miles (4km) to where double track extended. Beyond here it was single-line. In September 1908 passenger trains continued to Linefoot, but the service ran for only two months. The line was used in the early 20th century for excursions from Cleator Moor and Workington to Carlisle, worked by FR locomotives.

The single-line connection at Cloffocks to the LNWR Cockermouth & Workington line at Workington Bridge involved a curving bridge of iron spans on stone piers over the River Derwent, and it was opened in 1885. Its function was largely duplicated by the Calva Junction–Linefoot branch. In view of the desire of the C&WJ to avoid connection with the LNWR, its purpose is obscure. As it happened, the curve was little used and was abandoned at an early date.

Harrington & Lowca Light Railway

One of the branches authorised in the C&WJ Act in 1876 ran south-west from Harrington Junction for about 1½ miles (2.4km) to Rose Hill where it joined an existing mineral railway which climbed from Harrington Harbour at 1 in 15 and 1 in 17 to Lowca colliery high above the cliffs overlooking the sea. It was operated by the Workington Iron & Steel Co, and its opening date has eluded research. The new C&WJ branch, opened about 1877, joined the mineral line at Bain's Tramway Junction at the top of the 1 in 15 from the harbour and at the foot of the 1 in 17 climb. The harbour connection continued in use until the late 1920s.

In 1911 it was decided to operate a passenger service to Lowca. Stations were built at Rose Hill, Copperas Hill, Micklam, and Lowca; the line was reconstructed to conform to the requirements of the Light Railways Act, and in May 1912 application was made for the Harrington & Lowca Light Railway Order. Following its confirmation on 16 May 1913, a passenger service was introduced between Seaton on the Calva Junction–Linefoot section, through Workington Central, to Lowca, mainly for miners. From February 1922 it was terminated at Workington Central from where it ran until 1926. The Lowca trains, operated by the FR, had the distinction of working over the steepest adhesion-worked gradient on any British passenger railway.

Lowca colliery, known as Harrington No 10, was also served by a steeply-graded branch from the WCE Distington–Parton line, opened in 1879. The colliery closed on 26 July 1968, but coal traffic to the washery continued until May 1973 via Harrington and Parton.

Although the C&WJ was worked by the FR which supplied locomotives and rolling stock, it did possess some locomotives of its own, mainly 0–6–0 saddle tanks, used for shunting and short-distance hauls, and a stock of mineral wagons. At the end of 1922 there were 6 locomotives and 264 wagons. The C&WJ maintained its separate existence until grouping on 1 January

1923 when it became part of the LMS.

The first section to be closed completely was the Distington–Rowrah branch, in 1938, and it was dismantled the following year. The Calva Junction–Linefoot section followed, having lost its last passenger trains, to Seaton, in 1922. Traffic east of Buckhill colliery ended in 1935 at the same time as the closure of the Maryport & Carlisle Brigham branch, but trains to the colliery from Calva Junction continued until 1939. The track remained, and in 1991 was still used about twice a week to serve a naval establishment near Great Broughton. Seaton closed to freight in 1964.

The Moor Row–Siddick passenger service ended in 1931, on the same day as the Moor Row–Marron Junction service, but freight and occasional excursions ran until BR days. The line was closed as a through route in 1964, but Workington Central remained open for freight traffic from Siddick Junction until 1964.

Plates 21 and 22. *Above*: WD 2–8–0 No 90675 taking water at Longridge station on 28 August 1964 before working the freight back to Preston. *Below*: Southbound express diverted over the Whelley Loop to avoid Wigan crossing Douglas viaduct on Sunday 7 April 1968. (*John Marshall*)

Plates 23 and 24. *Above*: 2–6–4 tank No 42572 on a train from Manchester Central after arrival at Wigan Central on 26 August 1960. *Below*: Class 5 4–6–0 No 45014 on Skipton–Morecambe train leaving Lancaster Green Ayre, having just crossed the River Lune, 23 June 1962. The line was electrified at 6600V 50 Hz. (*John Marshall*)

CHAPTER 8

Cumbria, North

The Cockermouth & Workington Railway

The first link in the chain of lines connecting west Cumbria with Penrith and County Durham was a local railway of 8½ miles (13.7km) from the Whitehaven Junction Railway at Workington to Cockermouth. The Cockermouth & Workington Railway Company was incorporated in 1845 and the double-track line was opened in 1847. Its main function besides passenger facilities was the carriage of agricultural produce, and coal from a colliery near Camerton. In the same year as its incorporation, the company was drawing up plans for the extension of the railway to Keswick and in 1846 the extension was authorised by the C&W Railway Extension Act, but the C&W carried out no work on this extension.

The poet William Wordsworth, who was born in Cockermouth in 1770 but who had lived at Rydal near Ambleside since 1813, bitterly opposed the railway, and to his death in 1850 remained unreconciled to this invasion by trains into his beloved Lake District.

No heavy engineering was required; the line kept to the flat floor of the Derwent valley, but to maintain a fairly direct course it was compelled to cross the river five times by iron spans on stone piers. There were stations at Brigham, Broughton Cross, Camerton and Workington Bridge. (See map, page 114 and Plate 29.)

The line was operated as a purely local concern until the opening in 1865 of the Cockermouth, Keswick & Penrith Railway, which from its opening was worked by the LNWR. The C&W now found that it had become an important part of the

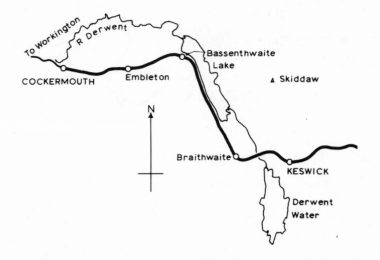

route from County Durham to Workington, an obvious asset to the LNWR. At the same time, in 1865, the Furness Railway was preparing to absorb the Whitehaven & Furness Railway, so gaining control of the entire route between Carnforth and Whitehaven. Only the Whitehaven Junction separated it from the Maryport & Carlisle at Maryport, so to block any attempt by the Furness to gain control of an alternative route between Carnforth and Carlisle, the LNWR presented Bills in 1865 for the absorption of the Cockermouth & Workington and the Whitehaven Junction. Both lines were amalgamated with the LNWR from 1866.

For operating its traffic the C&W possessed five locomotives, all different. Nos 2 and 3 were 0–4–2s; No 1, which replaced the first locomotive of 1847, was a 0–4–0 tank; No 4 was a 2–4–0, and No 5 a 0–6–0. They were taken into LNWR stock as Nos 1573–7 in 1867. All except the last were soon broken-up or sold. The 0–6–0 became LNWR No 1573 and was scrapped in 1881.

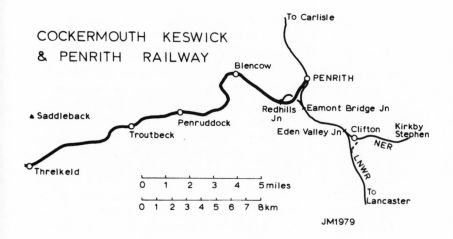

The Cockermouth, Keswick & Penrith Railway

The attempt by the Cockermouth & Workington to extend its line to Keswick in 1846 came to nothing, mainly because the district offered so little traffic. But when the Stockton & Darlington Railway (South Durham & Lancashire Union and Eden Valley) route was authorised to Clifton, south of Penrith, in 1857–8, then a line between Cockermouth and Penrith at once offered prospects of considerable traffic.

The Cockermouth, Keswick & Penrith Railway Company was incorporated in 1861 and construction began in May 1862. A further Act in 1863 gave powers to the LNWR and the Stockton & Darlington Railway companies to subscribe to the CK&P and to enter into working and traffic arrangements.

The South Durham & Lancashire Union and Eden Valley lines became part of the Stockton & Darlington in 1862, which in turn was amalgamated with the North Eastern Railway in 1863. By the time the CK&P was opened throughout in 1865, it was with the NER that it made contact at Penrith for the operation of the coke and iron traffic.

127

By the NER Eden Valley Junction branch, opened in 1873, both the NER and the CK&P joined the LNWR with north-facing junctions. To avoid a reversal at Penrith the NER built a connecting line from Eamont Junction on the LNWR to Redhills Junction on the CK&P, which gave through running for NER trains from County Durham to Workington and Whitehaven. The 'Redhills Curve', as this connection became known, was opened in 1866.

From the outset the CK&P was worked by the LNWR, which operated all the passenger trains and the local goods trains, but the mineral trains to and from County Durham were worked by NER locomotives to Workington. The CK&P maintained its independence until the grouping on 1 January 1923.

At Cockermouth a new station was built and the CK&P joined the Workington line west of the old C&W station. With the opening of the line to passengers on 2 January 1865 the C&W station became a goods station. As built, the line was single track throughout from the junction at Cockermouth. There were stations at Blencow, Penruddock, Troutbeck, Threlkeld, Keswick, Braithwaite, Bassenthwaite and Embleton. Single-line working continued throughout the period of intensive mineral traffic and it was not until 1900 that, because of the increase in summer passenger traffic, the sections from Redhills Junction to Blencow and Penruddock to Threlkeld were doubled. Other sections would have involved such heavy excavation and other engineering that they remained single.

The CK&P was one of the great scenic railways of England. In its 30¾ miles (49.5km) it gave the passenger views of mountains, Bassenthwaite Lake, the deep, wooded valley of the Greta and a wide open landscape with distant hills between Threlkeld and Blencow. From a height of 134ft (41m) at Cockermouth it climbed on gradients of 1 in 70–75 to a summit of 315ft (96m) at Embleton, fell to Bassenthwaite Lake and from a height of about 300ft (91m) at Keswick it climbed on gradients including 4 miles (6.4km) of 1 in 62½ to a summit of 886ft (270m) just beyond Troutbeck, from where it dropped to 650ft (198m) at Penrith on gradients including 4 miles of 1 in 70. Besides considerable rock cuttings, engineering works included nine iron bridges over the Greta between Keswick and Threlkeld and the Mosedale viaduct between Threlkeld and Troutbeck, 404ft (123m) long with twelve arches of 30ft (9.1m).

At Keswick a commodious station was built, with three platforms and quite elegant buildings in slate and stone. Immediately adjoining the station the company built a fine hotel in the same style, opened in 1864, with a conservatory connection to the down platform. Cockermouth station also had three platforms but had none of the elegance of Keswick. Other stations had buildings of nondescript styles.

At the opening of the line there were three daily passenger trains each way between Penrith and Workington, on weekdays only. By the 1880s this had increased to five each way on weekdays and two on Sundays, with additional trains between Keswick and Cockermouth, and Cockermouth and Workington. In the early 1900s this had become six on weekdays and one on Sundays. Connections were shown at Penrith to and from Darlington and in 1911–14 a through service was run in summer, but later this was changed to London Euston, with through carriages to Keswick and Workington on the 1030 from Euston and the 0915 from Workington. This service became the Keswick portion of the Lakes Express.

In 1913 the CK&P carried 482,006 passengers. By 1920 the total had dropped to 361, 526. After World War II, with increasing car usage, traffic declined until in 1960 it was reported that less than 20 per cent of Keswick's visitors arrived by train. Visitors to the Lake District were becoming less and less dependent on the railways to Keswick, Windermere and Coniston.

The introduction of diesel mutltiple-units on 3 January 1955 reduced the journey time from Penrith to Cockermouth from 70–77 min to 53–68 min, and eastwards from 78–85 min to 59–62 min. The fastest trains were those not requiring long crossing stops. Following introduction of the dmu service Blencow station, closed on 3 March 1952, was re-opened on 2 July 1956. The Workington portion of the Lakes Express, up to Penrith in the morning and down in the afternoon, became the only remaining steam working. The summer Sunday Newcastle–Keswick buffet-car train became a diesel multiple-unit with buffet facilities. Much of the local freight traffic was provided by the quarries of the Threlkeld Granite Company and the Flusco quarry and limeworks between Blencow and Penruddock.

For over seventy years from their introduction in 1880, the principal locomotives on the CK&P were the Webb 0–6–0 Cauliflowers, illustrated in Plate 30, which worked passenger and goods trains alike, gradually taking-over from the Ramsbottom DX 0–6–0s, but in the course of its life the line saw numerous other LNWR types, chiefly 2–4–2 and 0–6–2 tanks. Following strengthening of some of the iron bridges between Keswick and Threlkeld and elsewhere, Class 5, Jubilee, and even Royal Scot 4–6–0s were used on through services, though in the latter days of steam power the Class 2 2–6–0s were most common. Over a long period the NER mineral trains were hauled by Worsdell 0–6–0s of NER class P.

In the mid-1920s the decline of the Durham coke traffic brought an end to the through trains from the NER and the Redhills curve was taken out of use, though the track was not removed until the end of 1936. Beyond Cockermouth the section to Brigham was reduced to single track.

The end of the line came as a result of the Beeching 're-shaping'. The first portion of the through route to go was from Workington to Keswick, which closed to goods in 1964 and to passengers in 1966. Keswick to Penrith survived a little longer.

From 4 December 1967 it became a long single-track 'siding'. Stations were reduced to unstaffed halts from 1 July 1968. Passenger trains were withdrawn from 6 March 1972 and the Flusco Quarry traffic from 19 June. One may wonder what would be Wordsworth's reaction today were he to see the endless procession of heavy lorries, cars and caravans hurtling along the new road between Keswick and Workington, which now covers much of the trackbed of this once delightful scenic branch line.

The Maryport & Carlisle Railway

The Maryport & Carlisle Railway, with a total route length of only 42¾ miles (68.8km) ranked as one of our smallest systems. However, it was a profitable little concern; after 1856 dividends never fell below 4½ per cent and in 1873 they reached 13 per cent. The main line was 28 miles (45km) long and the two branches with which we are concerned made up the rest. At the 1923 grouping it owned twenty-eight tender and five tank locomotives. Traffic consisted largely of coal and iron, of which it carried enormous quantities.

Mealsgate Loop

In 1862 the company obtained powers to construct two branches: the Bolton branch from Aspatria to Mealsgate and the Wigton branch continuing from Mealsgate to rejoin the main line at Aikbank Junction near Wigton, total length 7¾ miles (12.5km). The main object was to develop a coalfield in the Bolton area. There were no heavy engineering works on the loop and it was opened for goods traffic in 1866. Passenger services at first ran only between Aspatria and Mealsgate, and it was 1878 before they were extended to Wigton. Intermediate stations were at Baggrow on the Aspatria–Mealsgate section and High Blaithwaite between Mealsgate and Aikbank Junction. Traffic on this section was light and it was closed entirely in 1921. The Aspatria–Mealsgate passenger service succumbed in the depression in 1930 but the goods traffic survived until 1952.

Bullgill–Brigham branch

This line formed a continuation northwards of the Whitehaven, Cleator & Egremont extension opened in 1866 to Marron East Junction on the Cockermouth & Workington

131

Railway. By running along 2 miles (3.2km) of what was by then LNWR track to Brigham, the mineral traffic could then turn up the M&C branch to Bullgill and along the main line to Carlisle. From 1869, with the opening of the Solway Junction Railway, it could turn off again at Brayton beyond Aspatria and so reach Scotland.

Powers for construction of the Brigham, or Derwent, branch were obtained in 1865. Construction was rapid, and the 6-mile (9.7km) line was opened in 1867. Although it passed through fairly hilly country and was steeply-graded, there was little heavy excavation and no major engineering apart from the girder bridge over the Derwent at Brigham. Stations were opened at Dearham, where there was a colliery, and Papcastle.

A passenger service of six trains on weekdays and three on Sundays was run between Maryport and Cockermouth, which involved reversing the trains at Bullgill and Brigham. For this purpose the M&C obtained running powers over the LNWR between Brigham and Cockermouth. Papcastle was a 'signal stop'. There was also a private station at Dovenby Lodge between Papcastle and Dearham for the use of the occupants of Dovenby Hall, through whose land the line ran.

The opening of the northern extension of the Cleator & Workington Junction Railway from Calva Junction near Workington to a junction with the Bullgill–Brigham branch at Linefoot brought additional mineral traffic to the northern end of the branch. A station was opened at Linefoot and for two months, from September to November 1908, it enjoyed a passenger service. Linefoot goods station remained in use until 1921. Excursion trains were occasionally run from Cleator Moor and Workington Central by this route. Freight traffic declined during the 1920s as on all the Cumbrian lines, but the passenger service survived until 1935 when the line was closed entirely, together with the C&WJ east of Buckhill Colliery.

North British Railway: Carlisle–Port Carlisle–Silloth

To avoid the difficult and treacherous navigation of the Solway Firth and the River Eden up into Carlisle, an Act was obtained in 1819 for a canal from Carlisle to join the Solway at Fisher's Cross near Bowness, the highest point which seagoing vessels could reach, and there to establish a new port called Port Carlisle.

The canal was opened in 1823 and was used to transport coal, lime and general merchandise to Carlisle. From the entrance basin to Carlisle it rose 70ft (21.3m) by nine locks. A steamer service was operated between Port Carlisle and Liverpool. In 1829 it enjoyed the distinction of transporting the dismantled *Rocket* of Robert Stephenson on its way to the Liverpool & Manchester Railway.

The opening of the Newcastle & Carlisle Railway in 1836 enabled Carlisle to obtain many of its requirements, including coal, quicker and more easily than by the canal. A branch to the canal basin at Carlisle was opened in 1837 and this was used for a time for exporting coal to Ireland. In the same year the Maryport & Carlisle Railway was authorised, and on opening in 1845 it provided much better shipping facilities at Maryport than were obtainable at Port Carlisle. Traffic on the canal declined until in 1853 it was closed.

There must still have been prospect of traffic, for in that year powers were obtained by the Port Carlisle Dock & Railway Act to convert the canal into a railway. Work was quickly carried out and the single-line railway was opened in 1854. The line was laid in the bed of the canal. The first 6 miles (9.5km) out of Carlisle were a succession of sharp reverse curves which required check rails. It then followed a dead straight course to Drumburgh where it turned north-westwards to Port Carlisle. Stations were built at Kirkandrews (Plate 31), Burgh by Sands, Drumburgh, Glasson and Port Carlisle.

Silting-up of the channel to Port Carlisle rendered the harbour practically useless, and in 1855 powers were obtained for an extension of the railway from Drumburgh to a new dock near Silloth Bay, much closer to the open sea.

From the opening to Silloth in 1856 the Drumburgh–Port Carlisle section became a branch which for many years was operated by the famous horse-drawn 'dandy' which is now preserved in the National Railway Museum at York. This particular vehicle ran from 1859 until 1914, by which time it was the last horse-drawn passenger vehicle on a British railway. Between January and May 1899 the branch was rebuilt for locomotive power, but the horse dandy continued to run the passenger service.

The original section from Carlisle to Port Carlisle continued to be operated by the Port Carlisle Railway & Dock Co, and the Drumburgh–Silloth section by the Carlisle & Silloth Bay Railway & Dock Co, until 1862 when both companies were leased to the NBR. Full amalgamation with the NBR took place in 1880.

Silloth became a popular holiday resort for Carlisle, and, until closure of the railway, vast numbers of people travelled there by train in the summer. Considerable freight traffic was carried to and from Silloth dock. The branch was distinguished by being the first in Britain to have its steam passenger services entirely replaced by diesel multiple-units, on 29 November 1954, only five months after their introduction between Leeds and Bradford.

The Silloth branch found further use during the period of operation of the Solway Junction Railway. The section from the Solway viaduct joined at Kirkbride, and at Abbey Town the southern section turned off (see below).

Train services on the Port Carlisle branch ended in 1932 and the line was abandoned. Despite the heavy summer passenger traffic, for much of the year Silloth traffic was light, and in its 22½ miles (36km) the railway served only one or two tiny villages. Had Silloth been on a branch from the M&C at Wigton the service might have survived, but the M&C could hardly be expected to feel drawn to a port rivalling its own at Maryport.

For many years from opening there were only four or five

daily trains each way, with two to and from Port Carlisle. After World War I a non-stop train ran each way on Thursday and Saturday and another ran through between Carlisle and Newcastle. Following the introduction of diesel multiple-units the service was increased to eight on weekdays, nine on Saturdays, and three on Sundays in summer. The Sunday trains were second-class only, and stopped only at Abbey Town. Much of the freight to and from Silloth was transferred to road haulage in 1960 when BR announced withdrawal of freight services, and in 1964 the line was closed completely.

The Solway Junction Railway

The story of the Solway viaduct has been admirably told by John Thomas in *Forgotten Railways: Scotland*; all we are concerned with are the sections within north-west England from Bowness on Solway to the M&C at Brayton.

The railway was projected as a link between the haematite ore mines of Cumbria and the furnaces of Lanarkshire, avoiding the long detour via Carlisle. The route as finally authorised in 1867 left the M&C at Brayton, joined the Silloth line at Abbey Town, left it again at Kirkbride, crossed the Solway between Bowness and Annan and joined the Caledonian main line at Kirtlebridge.

It was opened to goods traffic in September 1869, and to passengers in July 1870 with a service of three daily trains between Kirtlebridge and Brayton. The CR acquired the Kirtlebridge–Annan section in 1873 and the whole line was transferred to the CR in 1895. Mineral traffic enjoyed a brief period of prosperity, after which the line simply faded away and all traffic ended in 1921. The viaduct was not demolished until 1934–5. The work took nineteen months and it cost the lives of three young men who were drowned when the boat in which they were working on the demolition was swept away by the tide. (See Plate 32) Today one has to look hard in the flat country south of the Solway to find traces of the railway.

Gazetteer

The purpose of this gazetteer is to give fuller details of Acts of Parliament and dates of opening and closure of lines and stations, so relieving the text of fine detail, also to point out remaining features of interest, with Ordnance Survey map references, facilities for their inspection, and possibilities for walking stretches of line. The lines are dealt with in their order in the book, under chapter numbers. Numbers in brackets after the dates of the Acts of Parliament are the 'chapter numbers' of the Acts. Because many different railway Acts, some running to hundreds of pages, might receive the Royal Assent on the same day the date alone is insufficient reference. Chapter numbers on Acts and in the *Index to the Local and Personal Acts* (HMSO) are given in Roman numerals. The ordinary intelligent researcher has no difficulty with these, so Arabic numerals are used here to save space: eg, 387 instead of ccclxxxvii. The *Index* also gives regnal years. From the following key dates the year can easily be found:

11 Geo 4 & 1 Will 4	1830	63 & 64 Vic	1900
1 & 2 Will 4	1831	1 Ed 7	1901
7 Will 4 & 1 Vic	1837	10 Ed 7 & 1 Geo 5	1910
1 & 2 Vic	1838	1 & 2 Geo 5	1911

CHAPTER 1: IN AND AROUND MANCHESTER

BOLTON–LEIGH–KENYON JUNCTION
ACTS: 31 March 1825 (18); 14 May 1829 (36); 30 July 1831 (11); 20 May 1836 (52); incorporation in Grand Junction Co, 8 August 1845 (198); incorporation in LNWR, 16 July 1846 (204); widenings and improvements, 22 July 1878 (182); 6 August 1880 (145).
OPENED: Bolton–Leigh *(gds)* 1 August 1828; Leigh–Kenyon Junction *(gds)* 1 January 1831; Kenyon Junction–Bolton *(pass)* 13 June 1831; double-track deviations at Daubhill and Chequerbent and doubling between these, 2 February 1885; doubling Atherton–Atherton (Howe Bridge N) Junction, 4 July 1880; –Pennington Junction, 31 May 1880; –Kenyon Junction, 1 September 1864 (with opening of line from Tyldesley).

CLOSURES: Bolton Deansgate goods branch, 25 February 1930; Kenyon Junction–Bolton *(pass)* 29 March 1954; Howe Bridge North Junction–Pennington Junction *(gds)* 17 June 1963; remaining sections of original Daubhill line, 11 May 1964; Bolton Crook Street yard, 26 April 1965; Hulton's Siding–Bolton (remaining NCB traffic) 16 October 1967; Hulton's Siding–Howe Bridge East and West Junctions, 6 January 1969.

REMAINS: Bolton. Of the bridge over Crook Street only the south abutment remained in 1991. Bridge under Fletcher Street, 715083; bridge under Rothwell Street, 714082; both cast-iron girder type with stone parapets. Covered way 243yd (222m) under Bridgeman Street and High Street, in blue bricks with segmental arch. Course of 1885 line walkable (through quantities of household rubbish) to Daubhill where it joins the 1828 route. This can be followed back to the site of the former Daubhill station, 705076 (closed 2 February 1885). After closure, the top of the incline was built up to allow formation of a coal yard with hoppers beneath. From here down to High Street the incline was built over with streets of terraced houses about 1900. Near Chequerbent the track bed is cut across by the M61. At the A6 crossing, 675061, a crossing-keeper's house is still occupied, and recently extended. At Chequerbent incline top, 674059, are remains of old engine house foundations and stone block sleepers. Track walkable to Kenyon Junction but several underbridges gone, including the bridge over the Leeds & Liverpool Canal at Leigh. At Kenyon Junction part of the west-north curve can be traced at 645965.

USES: Crook Street yard, Bolton, is now an industrial estate. The site of Great Moor Street station is now a leisure pool and supermarket, both opened in 1988.

ECCLES–TYLDESLEY–WIGAN AND
TYLDESLEY–LEIGH–PENNINGTON JUNCTION

ACTS: LNWR, 11 July 1861 (130); Atherton West Junction (Howe Bridge N–W): LNWR, 6 August 1880 (145).

OPENED: Eccles–Tyldesley–Wigan; Tyldesley–Leigh–Pennington Junction, 1 September 1864; Howe Bridge N–W Junctions, January 1883.

CLOSURES: Tyldesley–Bolton *(pass)* 4 May 1942; Ellenbrook station, 2 January 1961; Howe Bridge, 20 July 1959; Hindley Green and Platt Bridge, 1 May 1961; Tyldesley–Wigan *(pass)* 1 January 1968 (Springs Branch Junction, Wigan, to Parsonage colliery, Leigh, still used for coal traffic); Eccles–Tyldesley–Leigh–Pennington Junction–Kenyon Junction (*all traffic*) 3 May 1969.

REMAINS: Near Patricroft the M602 has obliterated part of the track where it was crossed by the Patricroft–Clifton branch. From Monton the track bed is walkable along an embankment through pleasant wooded cuttings to Ellenbrook and then embankments and cuttings to Tyldesley and Leigh. At 741018 the East Lancashire Road Bridge (1930) covers about 100yd (90m) of the track. Underbridges are removed and some embankments tapered off. Tyldesley–Wigan: sections of embankment remain in uninteresting country.

USES: At Tyldesley station the ground has been landscaped and planted. At Leigh all steel underbridges are removed and the northern half of the viaduct (with chimneys) is used for enclosed spaces. The southern half of the viaduct has been demolished and the course of the line covered by industrial development. From the A572 to Pennington Junction the embankment has been cleared away and the course of the line and the flyover have been made into a park. On the Tyldesley–Wigan section from Platt Bridge to Springs Branch Junction, Wigan, a single track is still used for coal traffic.

PENNINGTON JUNCTION–PLATT BRIDGE
ACTS: LNWR, 6 August 1880 (145); 18 July 1881 (141); Pennington flyover, 20 July 1896 (149).
OPENED: Pennington Junction–Platt Bridge (*gds*) 9 February 1885; Pennington flyover (*pass* Leigh–Platt Bridge–Wigan, and Plank Lane station) 1 October 1903.
CLOSURES: Tyldesley–Leigh–Wigan (*pass*) 4 May 1942; Pennington–Bickershaw colliery junction last used about September 1963 (last passenger train, special, 21 September 1963). Plank Lane station closed 22 February 1915.
REMAINS: Short piece of embankment in Pennington Flash.
USES: At Pennington the whole area has been landscaped and made into a park. Beyond Pennington Flash, Bickershaw, colliery waste is tipped over the track. From Bickershaw colliery to Platt Bridge a single line is used for coal traffic.

ROE GREEN JUNCTION–BOLTON
ACTS: LNWR, 5 July 1865 (333); 12 July 1869 (115).
OPENED: Roe Green Junction–Little Hulton (*gds*) 1 July 1870;

New station at Bolton, Great Moor Street, 28 September 1874; Little Hulton–Bolton (*gds*) 16 November 1874; Roe Green Junction–Bolton (*pass*) 1 April 1875.

CLOSURES: Roe Green Junction–Bolton (*pass*) 29 March 1954; (*gds*) January 1961; Bolton–Little Hulton Junction–Little Hulton Colliery, 11 May 1964.

REMAINS: Track walkable from Roe Green Junction to the M61. At Bolton the covered way (cast-iron beams and jack arches) between Lever Street and Bridgeman Street is filled up.

USES: Plodder Lane shed site is now a housing estate.

MANCHESTER LIVERPOOL ROAD STATION

ACT: L&M, 14 May 1829 (35).

OPENED: 15 September 1830; public traffic began on 17 September.

CLOSED: (*pass*) 4 May 1844; (*gds*) 8 September 1975.

REMAINS: Station offices fronting on to Liverpool Road, 830979; passenger platform and booking office at rail level on first floor; goods warehouses; steel bridge of 1904 over Water Street; stone arch bridge over River Irwell, 828979.

USES: The station was restored for the Liverpool & Manchester Railway 150th anniversary in September 1980, after which it became the Greater Manchester Museum of Science and Industry.

MANCHESTER CENTRAL STATION AND APPROACHES

ACTS: Manchester Central Station Branch, 27 June 1872 (57); Romiley–Bredbury Junction, 24 June 1869 (25); Manchester South District Railway, 5 August 1873 (222); 30 June 1874 (58); Cornbrook–Chorlton-cum-Hardy transferred to CLC, 1 October 1891.

OPENED: Romiley–Bredbury Junction (*gds*) 15 February 1875; (*pass*) 1 April 1875; Manchester South District, Cornbrook–Heaton Mersey Junction, 1 January 1880; Manchester Central station, 1 July 1880.

CLOSURES: Withington & West Didsbury and Heaton Mersey stations, 3 July 1961; South District local service, 2 January 1967; Romiley–Bredbury Junction, 6 March 1967; Manchester Central station, 5 May 1969.

REMAINS: Manchester Central station train shed, 836976; Midland Hotel, 838978; iron viaducts, 829976–834976; Bredbury (lower) tunnel 162yd (148m) 934913. Abandoned track beds walkable.

USES: Manchester Central station is now the Greater Manchester Exhibition and Event Centre (G-MEX).

MANCHESTER DEANSGATE GNR WAREHOUSE
ACT: GNR, 30 May 1895 (36).
OPENED: 1 July 1898.
CLOSED: 29 March 1954.
REMAINS: Warehouse still stands (1991); track still in place on ground level.
USES: Upper yard now a car park, approached by the former railway incline from Watson Street. Ground floor and first floor of warehouse also used as a car park.

MACCLESFIELD, BOLLINGTON & MARPLE RAILWAY
ACTS: MB&M Act, 14 July 1864 (204); vesting in Macclesfield Committee (MS&L and NSR) 25 May 1871 (38).
OPENED: (*pass*) 2 August 1869; (*gds*) 1 March 1870. Doubling completed 26 June 1871; extension to junction with NSR at Macclesfield (*gds*) 3 April 1871; (*pass*) 1 July 1873. Curve to LNWR at Middlewood, 26 May 1885.
CLOSED: Middlewood spur to LNWR, 20 February 1955. Middlewood Higher station, 7 November 1960; Marple Wharf Junction–Macclesfield Goods Junction (*gds*) 5 August 1968. MB&B goods station–junction at Macclesfield (*gds*) 22 September 1969; Rose Hill–Macclesfield (*pass*) 5 January 1970.
REMAINS: Almost the entire trackbed from Rose Hill, 950888, to north of Macclesfield. High Lane station 944856: buildings demolished; south-bound platform now a picnic area. Higher Poynton station 944833: another picnic site. Buildings demolished but platforms remain. Bollington viaduct 930780.
USES: The track from Rose Hill to the outskirts of Macclesfield is now the Middlewood Way, opened to Bollington in 1985 and to Macclesfield in 1988, a ten-mile route for walkers, cyclists and horse riders. The nearby Macclesfield canal forms an alternative route out or back.

NEW MILLS–HAYFIELD
ACTS: Sheffield, Ashton-under-Lyne & Manchester (Whaley Bridge & Hayfield Branches) 27 July 1846 (230); Manchester, Sheffield & Lincolnshire (Newton & Compstall Branches) 28 June 1858 (75); Marple, New Mills & Hayfield Junction, 15 May 1860 (15); 28 April 1864 (7); amalgamation with MS&L, 5

Plates 25 and 26. *Above*: Lune viaduct, north of Sedbergh, on the LNWR Low Gill—Ingleton branch, 15 April 1977. *Below*: Coniston station, on 31 July 1954, with Class 2 2–6–2 tank No 41217 on a two-coach push-&-pull set forming the 20.22 train to Foxfield. (*John Marshall, W. A. Camwell*)

Plates 27 and 28. *Above*: Class 4F 0–6–0 No 44461 on a special to Ravenglass, formed of North Staffordshire Railway stock, at Moor Row on 3 August 1953. *Below*: Keekle viaduct, north of Cleator Moor, on the Cleator & Workington Junction Railway, 2 July 1979. (*W. A. Camwell, John Marshall*)

July 1865 (248); transfer to MS&L/Midland, 24 December 1869 (25); reservoir railway: Stockport Corporation, 1 August 1908 (48).

OPENED: Hyde Junction–Hyde, 1 March 1858; Hyde–Compstall, 5 August 1862; Compstall–New Mills, 1 July 1865; New Mills–Hayfield (*pass*) 1 March 1868; (*coal*) 7 April 1870; (*gds*) 18 March 1872.

CLOSED: New Mills–Hayfield: (*gds*) 15 April 1963; (*pass*) 5 January 1970.

REMAINS: New Mills tunnel, 198yd (181m) bricked-up at Hayfield end.

USES: Track in tunnel used as a siding. Remainder of route landscaped as a linear park and walk to Hayfield. All traces of Birch Vale and Hayfield stations have gone. At Hayfield a bus station and car park occupy the station site.

CHAPTER 2: EAST LANCASHIRE

THE EAST LANCASHIRE RAILWAY

ACTS: Clifton Junction–Bury–Rawtenstall, 4 July 1844 (60); extension to Accrington, Blackburn, Burnley and Colne, 30 June 1845 (35); change of name to ELR, 21 July 1845 (101); extension to Bacup, 27 July 1846 (276); Preston extension, 22 July 1847 (289); Skelmersdale branch, 18 August 1846 (381); 4 August 1853 (163); amalgamation with LYR, 13 August 1859 (110); widening Rawtenstall–Bacup, 24 July 1876 (170).

OPENED: Clifton Junction–Rawtenstall, 28 September 1846; Rawtenstall–Newchurch, 27 March 1848; Stubbins–Accrington N & W Junctions, 17 August 1848; Bamber Bridge and Lostock Hall Junctions–Preston (*pass*) 2 September 1850; (*gds*) November 1850; Newchurch–Bacup, 1 October 1852; Rawtenstall–Bacup widening, March 1881.

CLOSED: Molyneux Brow, 29 June 1931; Ringley Road, 5 January 1953; Radcliffe Bridge, 7 July 1958; Haslingden, 7 November 1960; Clifton Junction–Radcliffe N Junction; Rawtenstall–Bacup; Stubbins–Accrington, 5 December 1966; Bury–Rawtenstall (*pass*) 5 June 1972; Heywood–Bury–Rawtenstall (*gds*) 4 December 1980. (Re-opened by East Lancashire Railway Preservation Society: Bury–Ramsbottom 25 July 1987;–Rawtenstall 27 April 1991); Bamber Bridge–Preston (*pass*) 7 October 1968; (*gds*) May 1972; Lostock Hall Junction–Todd Lane Junction, 6 October 1969.

REMAINS: Clifton Junction EL platforms, 794028; Irwell viaduct, stone, thirteen arches including one of 96ft (29.2m) span over river, 80ft (24.4m) high, 792035; trackbed walkable through pleasant country, with footbridge over M62; bridge over Irwell, five iron arch spans, 70ft (21.3m) above river, 781067. From Stubbins, 792181, to Accrington some of the trackbed of the extension line makes a fine scenic walk. Alderbottom viaduct, 789192, over the Irwell was originally of timber and was rebuilt with three steel spans as late as 1892. Lumb viaduct, 789196, over the Irwell again, has nine stone arches of 40ft (12.1m) span, 65ft (19.8m) high, in a grand setting. Ogden viaduct, 784206. Helmshore station, 782211, still has signalbox, platforms, buildings, footbridge and wooden warehouse. Helmshore viaduct, 778218, below which is the Helmshore Industrial Museum in the old fulling mill. The track passes through bleak upland country. Through Haslingden the trackbed has been swallowed up by the A56 dual-carriageway trunk road; Haslingden tunnel (146yd/133.5m, 784236) has been opened out, 781228–784251. Baxenden bank, 2 miles (3.2km) drops down into Accrington on grades as steep as 1 in 38. The viaduct over the mill 'lodge', or pond, above Accrington has been removed. From Rawtenstall to Clough Fold the trackbed of the Bacup branch has been made into a road. Beyond, it is partly built over. From Waterfoot, 835216, it is walkable through all three tunnels in the gorge to east of Stacksteads, and is being made into a linear park. At Stacksteads are the remains of a level-crossing on a bridge over the Irwell.

The Preston extension north of Bamber Bridge and the adjacent course of the Walton Summit plateway make an interesting circular walk. Crossing-keeper's house, 557260. Todd Lane Junction station island platform, stationmaster's house and two-arch brick overbridge, 551264.

Parts of the Preston viaduct, converted into an embankment in 1884–6, can still be seen between the Ribble and the site of Whitehouse North Junction. The bridge over the Ribble carries a footpath. The original cast-iron bridge here was replaced by the steel spans in 1930.

USES: The Bury–Rawtenstall section is in use again and ELRPS will eventually run trains to Heywood. At Bacup the tunnel is used as a council grit store and the goods yard has become an industrial estate. Section of trackbed from Clifton, 790038, to Ringley Road, 775055, now a nature trail.

BURY–HOLCOMBE BROOK
ACTS: Bury & Tottington District Railways, 2 August 1877 (157); transfer to LYR, 24 July 1888 (140).
OPENED: 6 November 1882.
CLOSED: (*pass*) 5 May 1952; (*gds*) to Holcombe Brook, 2 May 1960; to Tottington, 19 August 1963.
REMAINS: Viaduct over Irwell at Bury, 802116. Viaduct over mill lodge at Tottington, 778135. Track walkable Bury to Tottington, but cutting at Brandlesholme Road, Bury, 796117, filled in.
USES: From Greenmount to Holcombe Brook the track is covered by housing. The site of Holcombe Brook station, 780151, is now a shopping precinct.

MIDDLETON JUNCTION–OLDHAM WERNETH
ACT: Manchester & Leeds Railway, 1 July 1839 (55).
OPENED: 31 March 1842.
CLOSED: (*pass*) 2 June 1958; (*gds*) 7 October 1963
REMAINS: A single line was left in from Middleton Junction to a coal depot at Chadderton. The track can be followed, but east of Broadway bridge, 902050, it has been landscaped.

BOLTON–BURY
ACTS: Liverpool & Bury Railway, 31 July 1845 (166); incorporating with Manchester & Leeds Railway, 27 July 1846 (282); Bradley Fold–Radcliffe: LYR, 18 July 1872 (116).
OPENED: Bolton–Bury, 20 November 1848; Bradley Fold–Radcliffe, 1 December 1879.
CLOSED: Darcy Lever station, 29 October 1951; Bradley Fold–Radcliffe North and South Junctions, 2 November 1964; Bolton–Bury, 5 October 1970.
REMAINS: Viaduct over St Peter's Way, Bolton, 726084, six 73ft (22.2m) lattice spans on stone piers, originally about 15ft (3m) higher until the road was built, when it crossed the Croal, now culverted, and the Manchester, Bolton & Bury canal. Viaduct over the Tonge at Darcy Lever, 734084, six lattice spans of 84ft (25.6m) and two of 54ft (16.4m) 86ft high. Stone viaduct of five spans of 73ft (22.25m) over the Irwell and canal at Bury, 795104.
USES: At the Bolton end all the formation has been removed and a supermarket occupies the site of the embankment adjacent to Burnden Park football ground, 723082.

LNWR CLIFTON BRANCH
ACTS: Liverpool & Manchester Railway, 21 July 1845 (123); bridge over Tyldesley line; LNWR, 6 August 1880 (145).
OPENED: 2 February 1850. Connection to Tyldesley line, 26 May 1884. (No Act.)
CLOSED: (*pass*) June 1850; (*gds*) 28 April 1953; Clifton Hall Sidings–Molyneux Junction, June 1961; connection to Tyldesley line, 31 May 1891.
REMAINS: From Monton Road, Eccles, 769993, to the East Lancashire Road, 779006, the course has been made into a 'linear walkway'. From the north end of the tunnel, 791019, to Clifton Junction station the track is walkable.
USES: At Patricroft the trackbed is occupied by industrial building and motorway. At Clifton it is used as a car park for industrial premises.

ROCHDALE–BACUP
ACTS: LYR, 30 June 1862 (97); 18 July 1872 (116).
OPENED: Rochdale–Facit (*gds*) 5 October 1870; (*pass*) 1 November 1870; Facit–Bacup, 1 December 1881.
CLOSED: Britannia station, 2 April 1917. Rochdale–Bacup (*pass*) and Facit–Bacup (*gds*) 16 June 1947; Bacup shed (26E) 10 October 1954; Whitworth-Facit (*gds*) 12 August 1963; Rochdale–Whitworth (*gds*) 12 August 1967.
REMAINS: Trackbed walkable from Wardleworth to Whitworth through interesting country. Tunnel 43yd (39m) under Whitworth Road, 895150; platform at Shawclough, 884150; 'double bridge', 881155; Healey Dell viaduct, 881160, in stone, eight spans of 30ft (9m) 105ft (32m) above the River Spodden.

North of Shawforth the track is again walkable, over the highest summit on the LYR, 965ft (294m) above sea level. Between here and Bacup is some fine masonry work; beyond Britannia tunnel, 144yd (132m) 875216, is the site of Bacup shed on the right.
USES: Between Whitworth and Facit, and at Shawforth, the trackbed is now part of housing estates. Site of Whitworth station now a road.

BLACKBURN–PADIHAM
ACTS: LYR, 18 May 1866 (44); extension to Rose Grove, 15 July 1867 (136).

OPENED: (*gds*) 1 June 1877; (*pass*) 15 October 1877.

CLOSED: (*pass*) 3 December 1957; (*gds*) 2 November 1964.

REMAINS: From Great Harwood Junction, Blackburn, to the Rishton–Great Harwood road the track offers the walker a choice of flooded cuttings or dull scenery. From here through Great Harwood cuttings are, or are being, filled-in and grassed. Beyond the Accrington–Whalley road, 747325, is a good walk in the Calder valley over Martholme viaduct, 752329, of ten stone spans of 40ft (12m) 65ft (19.8m) high. Several under-bridges have been removed. Beyond Simonstone a single line remains to serve Padiham power station.

USES: Commercial development of Great Harwood station site. Simonstone station yard still used as coal depot. Padiham station yard covered by industrial building.

STANDEDGE OLD TUNNELS AND MICKLEHURST LOOP

ACTS: Standedge tunnel: Huddersfield & Manchester Railway & Canal, 21 July 1845 (105); second Standedge tunnel: LNWR, 16 July 1866 (168); Loop: LNWR, 3 July 1879 (117).

OPENED: Standedge first tunnel, 1 August 1849; second tunnel, 12 February 1871; Micklehurst Loop (*gds*) 1 December 1885; (*pass*) 3 May 1886.

CLOSED: Micklehurst station, 1 May 1907; Staley & Millbrook station, 1 November 1909; Friezland and Uppermill stations, 1 January 1917; Micklehurst Loop, 7 September 1964; Stalybridge–Friezland (*gds*) 27 February 1965; old Standedge tunnels, 31 October 1966; Stalybridge–Millbrook (*gds*) 1975.

REMAINS: The whole route is worth visiting. Engineering works were carried out in blue brick, but the viaducts at Mossley and Friezland were demolished and cleared in 1975–6, probably to recover them. All steel bridges have been removed. At Stalybridge, where the line left the tunnel and crossed the River Tame and the canal on a viaduct, the engineering is impressive. Beyond here the track is walkable to Millbrook and from there to Mossley, giving good views of the older line across the valley. From Mossley to Greenfield the trackbed is being developed as a linear park. The short tunnel north of Micklehurst is now submerged beneath landscaping and road improvements. At Friezland landscaping has removed all trace of the railway. From Uppermill the track is walkable to Diggle. Track has been removed from the two single-line Standedge tunnels.

USES: Uppermill station area now occupied by housing, and Saddleworth swimming pool.

BRANCHES TO DELPH AND OLDHAM

ACTS: Huddersfield & Manchester Railway & Canal, 21 July 1845 (105) and 18 August 1846 (380).

OPENED: Greenfield–Delph, 1 September 1851; Greenfield–Oldham, 5 July 1856.

CLOSED: (*pass*) 2 May 1955; Greenfield–Delph (*gds*) 4 November 1963; Greenfield–Oldham (gds) 12 April 1964.

REMAINS: Delph branch walkable throughout and interesting scenically. On the Oldham branch the tunnel is walled-up at both ends. The cutting at the Greenfield end is overgrown and flooded. From the Oldham end, 968044, to Lees, 958045, the trackbed has been made into a linear park. From Lees to Oldham it is walkable through heaps of assorted domestic refuse.

USES: At Delph the station has become a private residence and a small 'railway museum' with inside-cylinder 0–6–0 saddle tank *Brookes No 1* (Hunslet 2387 of 1941) a brake van, oil tank wagon and a coach. These can be seen by the public with permission. Grotton station on the Oldham branch is a private residence.

OLDHAM–ASHTON-UNDER-LYNE

ACTS: OA&GBJR, 10 August 1857 (137); vesting in LNWR and MS&L, 30 June 1862 (48).

OPENED: (*pass*) 26 August 1861; (*gds*) 1 February 1863.

CLOSED: (*pass*) 4 May 1959; (*gds*) 22 May 1967.

REMAINS: From the 56yd (51m) Smallshaw 'tunnel' (covered way) at Ashton, 938998, northwards the track is walkable, part of it through pleasant country. Near Limehurst two embankments cross deep valleys, the northern one being 80ft (24m) high. At Park the course of a branch to Park Bridge Ironworks turns off right. Some small under-bridges have been removed.

USES: South of Smallshaw tunnel, Ashton, the trackbed is taken by industrial development.

CHAPTER 3: MERSEYSIDE

LIVERPOOL EDGE HILL TO CROWN STREET AND WAPPING

ACTS: Liverpool & Manchester, 5 May 1826 (49); second tunnel to Crown Street, 21 July 1845 (123); extension of Wapping goods yard: LNWR, 25 July 1864 (226); 18 July 1872 (87).

OPENED: Edge Hill–Crown Street, 15 September 1830; Edge Hill–Wapping, 16 September 1830, but not used until 1

December (experimentally) and January 1831 (regularly).

CLOSED: Crown Street station (*pass*) 15 August 1836; (*gds*) 1 May 1972; Wapping (Park Lane Goods) 1 November 1965.

REMAINS: Cutting at Edge Hill with steps and 'caves' cut into the sandstone, 367898; tunnels to Crown Street: small tunnel, 290yd (265m) long, 16ft 9in (5m) wide and 12ft (3.66m) high, now filled in at Crown Street end; entrance to Wapping tunnel, fenced off inside; large tunnel 124yd (113m) leading to a cutting and bridges under Crown Street, 365897; Crown Street yard is 'landscaped', with the Wapping tunnel shaft in the middle. At Wapping the entire goods yard is cleared. The lower end of Wapping tunnel is sealed-off. The old 1828 portal 346894 can be visited and seen through, but is gated. The other tunnel arches are bricked up.

USES: Edge Hill cutting and tunnels are being developed as a visitor centre. Part of Park Lane goods yard is used by a steel stockist.

LIVERPOOL EDGE HILL–WATERLOO–RIVERSIDE

ACTS: Liverpool & Manchester Railway, 21 July 1845 (123); Mersey Dock (various powers) 27 July 1893 (157).

OPENED: Edge Hill–Waterloo (*gds*) 1 August 1849; Riverside station, 12 June 1895.

CLOSED: Waterloo Dock goods station, 30 September 1963; Riverside station, 1 March 1971.

REMAINS: Entrance to Victoria tunnel seen from Edge Hill station, 371900; bottom end of Waterloo tunnel, 339914; Riverside station shed, 337905.

USES: Riverside station train shed houses road vehicles.

LIVERPOOL EXCHANGE STATION

ACTS: Original station: LYR, 3 August 1846 (312); new station, 24 July 1876 (170) 2 August 1883 (169).

OPENED: First station, 13 May 1850; new station, first half (north-east side) 12 December 1886; complete station, 2 July 1888.

CLOSED: 30 April 1977.

REMAINS: Portions of the approach viaducts of both old and new lines, 340912.

LIVERPOOL CENTRAL STATION

ACTS: Liverpool Central Railway, 29 July 1864 (290); transferring company to MS&L, GNR, and Midland companies, 30 July 1866 (294).

OPENED: 1 March 1874.

CLOSED: 17 April 1972.

REMAINS: Portion of retaining wall and tunnel entrance, 352900.

CLC NORTH LIVERPOOL LINES

ACT: Hunts Cross and Halewood East Junctions–Aintree and Huskisson: Cheshire Lines, 30 July 1874 (169).

OPENED: Hunts Cross and Halewood East Junctions–Walton-on-the-Hill and Aintree Junction, 1 December 1879. Walton-on-the-Hill–Huskisson (*gds*) 1 July 1880; (*pass*) 2 August 1880. Huskisson–Sandon Dock MR (*gds only*) 1 November 1882. Fazakerley–Alexandra Dock (MR line, *gds only*) 1 June 1885. Clubmoor station, 14 April 1927; Warbreck station, 1 August 1929.

CLOSED: Huskisson (*pass*) 30 April 1885; (*gds*) 1 January 1969. Walton-on-the-Hill (*pass*) 1 January 1918; (*gds*) 9 September 1968. Childwell station, 1 January 1931. Gateacre–Aintree (*pass*) 7 November 1960. Walton-on-the-Hill locomotive depot (8R) 15 December 1963 (closed to LMS locomotives October 1936). Remaining locomotives to Aintree (8L) shed. Huskisson (transferred to National Carriers Ltd) 1 January 1969. Fazakerley–Alexandra (Langton) Dock, MR, 5 January 1970. Aintree (*gds*) 7 December 1964. Gateacre (*pass*) 17 April 1972. Knotty Ash (*gds*) 1 May 1972.

REMAINS: Almost the entire trackbed is walkable, and interesting, with all underbridges still in place. It offers scope for linear park development. Gateacre station, 429879: platforms only. 'Cut-and-cover' tunnel, 84yd (77m) under roads, 407908, with second one on west side for future quadrupling. Several overbridges also have second spans for this purpose. Knotty Ash, 402915: platforms and ramp approaches. Attractive walk through sandstone cutting with five stone overbridges to beyond West Derby station, 395928. Here buildings survive with platforms and ramp approaches. Two modern steel through lattice-girder spans over roads, 382943 and 375951, the latter over the East Lancashire Road. Tunnel entrance blocked at Walton-on-the-Hill. Tunnels, 223yd (204m) 603yd (551m) and 229yd (209m). At Kirkdale, 350943, a blind tunnel on the east side, 150yd (137m) long, for possible future quadrupling (?). Bridge over LNWR Canada Dock branch (opened 15 October 1866) 350942. Aqueduct carrying Leeds & Liverpool Canal over, 345934.

Aintree Central station, 365978, platforms only.

USES: Knotty Ash and West Derby goods yards now contractors' depots. West Derby station buildings at street level: house occupied; offices now a fruit and vegetable shop. Walton-on-the-Hill: housing development covering goods yard and loco-motive depot area. The trackbed from Halewood through Knotty Ash and Fazakerley to Aintree has been made into the Liverpool Loop Line Cycle Route.

LIVERPOOL OVERHEAD RAILWAY
ACTS: MD&HB, 22 July 1878 (198); 10 August 1882 (204); LOR, 24 July 1888 (110); 20 June 1892 (112).
OPENED: Alexandra–Herculaneum, 6 March 1893; Alexandra–Seaforth Sands, 30 April 1894; Herculaneum–Dingle, 21 December 1896; LYR connection to Seaforth, 2 July 1905.
CLOSED: 31 December 1956.
REMAINS: Tunnel entrance above north corner of Herculaneum Dock, 355875; portion of embankment at Seaforth, 334966.

WIRRAL RAILWAY–SEACOMBE BRANCH
ACTS: Seacombe, Hoylake & Dee Side Railway, 18 July 1881 (115); amalgamation with Wirral Railway, 11 June 1891 (35).
OPENED: 1 June 1895.
CLOSED: (*pass*) 4 January 1960; (*gds*) 17 June 1963.
REMAINS: Overbridge at Seacombe, 323908.
USES: From Bidston the entire trackbed has been utilised as an approach to the new Wallasey road tunnels under the Mersey. The Seacombe & Egremont station site has been 'developed' with four-storey flats and a children's playground.

HOOTON–WEST KIRBY
ACTS: Hooton–Parkgate: Birkenhead Railway, 17 July 1862 (148); Hoylake Railway (extension) 16 July 1866 (186); Parkgate–West Kirby: LNWR, 12 July 1882 (129).
OPENED: Hooton–Parkgate, 1 October 1866; Parkgate–West Kirby, 19 April 1886; Kirby Park station, October 1894; Caldy station, May 1909.
CLOSURES: Parkgate, first station, 19 April 1886; Thurstaston and Caldy (*pass*) 5 July 1954; passenger service throughout, 17 September 1956; goods throughout, 7 May 1962.
REMAINS: Hadlow Road station, 331774, restored as a museum with a length of single track beside the up platform, level crossing gates, and signal box (rescued from Hassall Green on

the NSR Harecastle–Sandbach line); Neston rock cutting, 300774, nature reserve; original Parkgate station (1866): fragment of platform, 284779; second Parkgate station (1886): remains of subway; Thurstaston station, 238235: platforms.

USES: Whole route now Wirral Country Park, a 12-mile walk with rail access at Hooton and West Kirby. Visitor centre at Thurstaston station. Cycling not permitted.

CHAPTER 4: WEST LANCASHIRE

WEST LANCASHIRE RAILWAY, SOUTHPORT–PRESTON

ACTS: 14 August 1871 (200); 6 August 1872 (183); Tarleton branch, 3 June 1881 (57); transfer to LYR, 15 July 1897 (130).

OPENED: Hesketh Park–Hesketh Bank, 19 February 1878; Hesketh Park–Southport Windsor Road, 10 June 1878; Hesketh Bank–Tarleton (*gds*) 19 February 1881; Hesketh Bank–Longton, 18 May 1882; Southport Windsor Road –Central; Longton–Preston (*pass*) 4 September 1882; (*gds*) 15 February 1883; Penwortham and Ribble Junctions, Preston–Whitehouse South Junction (*pass*) 16 April 1883; (*gds*) 1 June 1883.

CLOSED: Preston WLR station (*pass*) 16 July 1900; Southport Windsor Road (*pass*) June 1902; Tarleton branch (*pass*) 10 October 1913; (*gds*) November 1930. Meols Cop (Southport)–Penwortham Junction, Preston; Whitehouse West–North Junctions, 7 September 1964; Preston WLR station Penwortham Junction–Whitehouse South Junction (*gds*) 26 January 1965.

REMAINS: As the line passed through flat country there were few earthworks and little remains of the trackbed except a cutting at Penwortham, the embankment from Penwortham Junction, 526278, to Whitehouse North and South Junctions, 539280 and 540276; arches north of the Ribble bridge, 532284, and some walling at the Preston station site, 530288.

USES: Much of the trackbed has returned to agricultural use. Hesketh Bank station site built over. In the cutting at Penwortham (the site of Penwortham Cop Lane Halt) the trackbed is now a road. Piers of bridge over Ribble, 531283, carry a pipe. Preston station site landscaped.

SOUTHPORT & CHESHIRE LINES EXTENSION

ACTS: Netherton–Birkdale, 11 August 1881 (193); Birkdale–

Southport Lord Street, 18 August 1882 (261).

OPENED: 1 September 1884; Barton & Halsall station, 5 April 1886 (renamed Mossbridge, 1894); Seaside station, 19 June 1901 (renamed Ainsdale Beach, 1911).

CLOSED: (*pass*) 7 January, (*gds*) 7 July 1952; Mossbridge, 1 January 1917.

REMAINS: Trackbed walkable from Netherton, 371006, to Woodvale, 313106.

USES: Aintree–Ainsdale: trackbed made into the Ainsdale Railway Path, an 8-mile cycle route. From Woodvale, 313106, to Southport, 320161, the trackbed has been made into a road.

LIVERPOOL, SOUTHPORT & PRESTON JUNCTION

ACTS: 7 August 1884 (226); transfer to LYR, 15 July 1897 (130).

OPENED: Meols Cop, Southport, –Barton (*pass*) 2 September 1887; Barton–Hillhouse Junction, 1 November 1887.

CLOSED: (*pass*) 26 September 1938; (*gds*) 21 January 1952.

REMAINS: Trackbed walkable, Blowick–Hillhouse Junction. Several stone overbridges.

GARSTANG & KNOTT END RAILWAY

ACTS: Garstang & Knot End Railway (*sic*) 30 June 1864 (149); Knott End Railway, 12 August 1898 (244).

OPENED: Garstang–Pilling, 5 December 1870; Pilling–Knott End, 1 August 1908.

CLOSED: Garstang–Knott End (*pass*) 31 March 1930; Pilling–Knott End (*gds*) 13 November 1950. Garstang Town–Pilling (*gds*) 1 August 1963; Garstang & Catterall–Garstang Town, 16 August 1965.

REMAINS: Much of trackbed walkable, but hardly worth the effort. Pilling, 414478, fragment of platform. At Knott End the station platforms remain, 346485, close to the ferry from Fleetwood.

USES: Garstang: section of route used as access road to new bridge over Wyre and water pumping station. Station yard is covered by a housing estate. The approach road is named 'Station Way', 491455. Nateby station house now a dwelling, 459461. Station yard used a coal depot. Pilling yard now small industrial estate: station house now a dwelling. Knott End station building is now a café.

PRESTON & LONGRIDGE RAILWAY

ACTS: 14 July 1836 (122); Fleetwood, Preston & West Riding

Junction Railway, 27 July 1846 (266); vesting in LNWR/LYR, 17 June 1867 (45).

OPENED: 1 May 1840; connection to Preston & Wyre Railway, 14 January 1850; Maudland Curve, Preston, 1 June 1885.

CLOSED: (*pass*) 2 June 1930; (*gds*) 6 November 1967.

REMAINS: Tunnels 146yd (133m) 272yd (249m) and 385yd (352m) in Preston; platforms at Deepdale, 545303; level-crossing house, 551305; Ribbleton station, 567320; Longridge station, 604374; tunnel under road, 612378; Longridge quarries. Trackbed much overgrown. Walkable near Grimsargh.

USES: Deepdale yard now coal concentration depot. Track still used to exchange sidings at junction with power station branch, 575327. Ribbleton station house now a dwelling. Longridge station now headquarters of local St John Ambulance Brigade; also used by a pigeon club. Beyond, the trackbed is now a road.

PRESTON & WALTON SUMMIT PLATEWAY

ACT: The plateway was not specifically included in any of the Lancaster Canal Acts, 1792 (101) 1793 (107) 1796 (97).

OPENED: 1 June 1803.

CLOSED: 1859; dismantled 1868.

REMAINS: Incline at Preston, 542287, now path in park; stretch of embankment and incline, 542285, to Todd Lane, 552269; several stone block sleepers still in place. An interesting and pleasant walk.

CHAPTER 5: BETWEEN BLACKBURN AND ST HELENS

BLACKBURN (CHERRY TREE) TO CHORLEY

ACTS: LYR, 25 July 1864 (270); vesting jointly in LYR and LUR, 26 May 1865 (21); vesting LUR in LNWR, 16 July 1883 (110).

OPENED: (*gds*) 1 November 1869; (*pass*) 1 December 1869.

CLOSED: (*pass*) 4 January 1960. Chorley–Feniscowles (*gds*) 3 January 1966; Feniscowles–Cherry Tree Junction (*gds*) 22 April 1968.

REMAINS: Most of the course is walkable and interesting. Stone viaduct, three arches, over Blackburn–Chorley road (A674) 649258. Feniscowles Station ruin, 648252; embankments, 84ft (25.6m) high, across Stock Clough Brook valley, 646243, and 83ft (25m) across Roddleworth Brook valley, 644236; Withnell station house, 638227; Brinscall station platforms, 627215; Heapey station house, 610196.

USES: Houses at Withnell and Heapley now residences.

ADLINGTON–BOARS HEAD
ACT: Lancashire Union Railways, 25 July 1864 (273).
OPENED: (*gds*) 1 November 1869; (*pass*) 1 December 1869.
CLOSED: Boars head, 31 January 1949; Red Rock (*pass*) 26 September 1949; (*gds*) 2 September 1957; through route (*pass*) 4 January 1960; (*gds*) 25 May 1971.
REMAINS: Most of trackbed walkable. Three-arch viaduct over Douglas, 601124; Lancaster Canal aqueduct, 586104; piers of Douglas viaduct, 584092.
USES: White Bear station yard, Adlington, now contractor's depot.

LYR HINDLEY–BLACKROD–HORWICH
ACT: 25 July 1864 (270).
OPENED: (*gds*) 15 July 1868; Hindley–Blackrod (*pass*) 14 September 1868; Blackrod–Horwich (*pass*) 14 February 1870; Horwich 'Fork' (*gds*) 20 June 1887, (*pass*) 1 July 1887.
CLOSED: Dicconson Lane & Aspull and Hilton House, 1 February 1954; through route, local passenger trains, 4 January 1960, through expresses, 9 September 1968; Horwich (*pass*) 27 September 1965; (*gds*) 25 April 1966. Branch still open Blackrod to Locomotion Industrial Estate, formerly Horwich Locomotive Works/British Rail Engineering. Horwich Fork Junction–Loco Junction, 30 January 1967.
REMAINS: Sections of trackbed walkable but uninteresting.
USES: Horwich station site, 640115, to Chorley New Road landscaped as part of recreation area.

WHELLEY LOOP: STANDISH–BAMFURLONG; HAIGH JUNCTION–WHELLEY JUNCTION
ACTS: Haigh Junction–Ince Moss Junction–St Helens: Lancashire Union Railways, 25 July 1864 (273); Standish Junction–Whelley Junction: LUR, 28 June 1877 (57); Platt Bridge Junction line (Amberswood West Junction–Bamfurlong Junction): LNWR, 16 July 1883 (110).
OPENED: Haigh Junction–Ince Moss Junction–St Helens (*gds*) 1 November 1869; Ince Moss Junction–Whelley (*pass*) 1 January 1872; Standish–Whelley Junction, 5 June 1882; Amberswood West Junction–Bamfurlong Junction, 25 October 1886.

CLOSED: Ince Moss Junction–Whelley (*pass*) 1 March 1872; Haigh Junction–Whelley Junction, 23 January 1967 (regular traffic ended 25 April 1965); Standish Junction–Bamfurlong Junction –no official closure date; track singled in 1972 after completion of electrification; went out of use during 1974.

REMAINS: Viaduct over River Douglas, 583088. From site of Haigh Junction, 585084, through the cutting (formerly Haigh tunnel) through the grounds of Haigh Hall, to the Leeds & Liverpool Canal at 600062 is an interesting walk.

ORMSKIRK–RAINFORD–ST HELENS

ACTS: Ormskirk–Skelmersdale: Liverpool, Ormskirk & Preston Railway, 18 August 1846 (381); extension to Rainford: ELR, 4 August 1853 (163); St Helens–Rainford: Liverpool & Manchester Railway, 21 July 1845 (123); St Helens Canal & Railway, 22 July 1847 (271) and 4 August 1853 (134).

OPENED: St Helens–Rainford, 1 February 1858; Ormskirk –Rainford, 1 March 1858.

CLOSED: Rainford Junction–St Helens (*pass*) 18 June 1951; (*gds*) 6 July 1964; Ormskirk–Rainford Junction (*pass*) 5 November 1956; Rainford Junction–Skelmersdale (*gds*) 16 November 1961; Ormskirk–Skelmersdale (*gds*) 4 November 1963.

REMAINS: Much of route walkable between Ormskirk and Rainford Junction, but uninteresting. Rainford Junction– Rainford village, good walk along embankment. From site of Rainford Village station, 478010, to Rookery station, 486003, the route has been made into 'Rainford Linear Park Phase 1'.

USES: Part of trackbed at Skelmersdale now incorporated into the A577 road. Housing covers course of line into Rainford Junction.

GLAZEBROOK TO WIGAN CENTRAL AND ST HELENS

ACTS: Glazebrook–Wigan: Wigan Junction Railway Acts, 16 July 1874 (117); 2 August 1875 (189); 17 June 1878 (97); MS&L, 2 August 1883 (157); Lowton–St Helens: St Helens & Wigan Junction, 22 July 1885 (121); change of name to Liverpool, St Helens & South Lancashire Railway: 26 July 1889 (91).

OPENED: Glazebrook–Strangeways (*gds*) 16 October 1879; (*pass*) 1 April 1884; Strangeways–Wigan, 1 April 1884; connections to Lancashire Union Railways, July 1880; Strangeways East Junction–Bickershaw Junction on LNWR Tyldesley line, 25 October 1886; extension to Wigan Central, 3 October 1892; Lowton St Mary's–St Helens (*gds*) 1 July 1895; (*pass*) 3 January

1900; connection from Golborne Junction–Edge Green, 22 April 1968.

CLOSED: Lowton St Mary's–St Helens (*pass*) 3 March 1952; Glazebrook–Wigan Central (*pass*) 2 November 1964; Haydock–St Helens (*gds*) 4 January 1965; Strangeways East Junction–Lowton St Mary's (*gds*) 5 April 1965; Glazebrook Moss Junction–Dam Lane Junction, 11 May 1965; Wigan Central Goods–Bickershaw Junction, 6 November 1967; Glazebrook West Junction–Lowton St Mary's–Edge Green Signal Box, 22 April 1968.

REMAINS: Portions of the trackbed on both lines remain, but much has disappeared completely under landscaping and redevelopment and no long section is walkable. In Wigan no trace remains. All has been landscaped or built over.

USES: About $2^1/_2$ miles (4km) of the St Helens branch from the 1968 connection from Golborne Junction, 605990, to Haydock, 565977, is used to serve the Shell UK Oil Haydock Terminal. From here a short stretch is made into a road.

CHAPTER 6: THE LUNE VALLEY

CLAPHAM–INGLETON–LOW GILL AND
WENNINGTON–LANCASTER–MORECAMBE

ACTS: Skipton–Low Gill and Clapham–Lancaster: North Western Railway, 26 June 1846 (92); Lancaster–Morecambe: Morecambe Harbour & Railway, 16 July 1846 (184); Lancaster Green Ayre–Castle: NWR, 24 May 1849 (19); Ingleton–Low Gill: Lancaster & Carlisle Railway, 25 August 1857 (161).

OPENED: Morecambe–Lancaster, 12 June 1848; Skipton–Ingleton, 30 July 1849; Lancaster–Wennington, 17 November 1849; Lancaster Green Ayre–Castle, 19 December 1849; Wennington–Bentham, 2 May 1850; Bentham– Clapham, 1 June 1850 (all single-line); Ingleton–Low Gill (*gds*) 24 August 1861; (*pass*) 16 September 1861; Scale Hall station, Lancaster, 8 June 1957.

DOUBLED: Hellifield–Hornby, autumn 1850; Clapham–Ingleton, 1 October 1861; Lancaster–Morecambe, 3 April 1877; Lancaster Green Ayre–Ladies Walk, 1880; Hornby–Ladies Walk, 3 March–27 October 1889.

CLOSED: Clapham–Ingleton, 1 June 1850. Reopened as double track, 1 October 1861. Middleton-on-Lune station, 13 April 1931; Clapham–Low Gill (*pass*) 1 February 1954; (*gds*) 19 June

1966; Hornby station, 16 September 1957; Caton station, 1 May 1961; Wennington–Lancaster (Green Ayre and Castle)–Morecambe (*pass*) 3 January 1966; (*gds*) 5 June 1967, except Lancaster Castle–Green Ayre (*gds*) 8 January 1968 but retained as link to Lancaster power station until this closed on 1 October 1976.

REMAINS: Clapham–Low Gill: Trackbed mostly walkable, though some sections have returned to agricultural use or private occupation. Ingleton viaduct, 693732, eleven arches faced in stone, fenced-off both ends. Cowan Bridge, 635766, viaduct of five segmental arches across Leck Beck, close to the house where the Brontë sisters lived while at school in 1824–5. Kirkby Lonsdale station, 629774, station house, weighbridge house. Stone arch over Barbon Beck, 630825. Stone arch over Luge Gill, 629871. Bowstring deck-girder span over River Rawthey at Brigg Flatts, 644909. Waterside viaduct over River Lune, 631931, cast-iron arch over river flanked by three stone arches each end. Low Gill viaduct, 616964, eleven stone arches, fenced-off both ends.

Wennington–Lancaster–Morecambe: Much of trackbed returned to agricultural use, but walkable Caton–Lancaster, and interesting. Bridge over River Hindburn, 599685, removed. Caton station, 530648: platforms, station house, level-crossing and goods shed. Five-span iron bridge over Lune, 522648; road overbridge and six-span iron bridge over Lune, 520648. Halton station, 504645: lattice-girder approach bridge from Halton village; station platforms, offices and goods shed on north side. Near site of Lancaster Green Ayre station the restored crane from Hornby goods shed has been erected, 479622.

USES: Ingleton Midland station site, 695730, now a community centre, car park and information office. LNWR station site, 690734, used as road material store. Kirkby Lonsdale station house now caters for bed and breakfast. Barbon station site, 630824, now small housing estate. Middleton-on-Lune station, 627883, and Sedbergh station, 643920, now occupied as dwellings. Hornby station, 585680, now small industrial estate. Caton station, 530648: house occupied; goods shed now a Roman Catholic church. Bridge over Lune, 476621, now rebuilt for new road. The trackbed has been converted into walks as follows: Caton Green–Lancaster, 6 miles; Lancaster–Morecambe, 3½ miles; Lancaster Green Ayre–Castle, ½ mile. Lancaster Green Ayre shed site now a supermarket and car park; station area: a landscaped riverside park.

Plates 29 and 30. Above: Workington Bridge station, closed 1 January 1951, on the LNWR Cockermouth–Workington section, 2 August 1954. The connection from Cloffocks Junction on the Cleator & Workington Junction Railway was behind the bank on the right and joined beyond the bridge. *Below*: Cauliflower 0–6–0 LMS No 28372 (LNWR 8372) at Bassenthwaite Lake station on the 14.10 Workington–Penrith train on 4 August 1947. (*W. A. Camwell*)

Plates 31 and 32. Above: Carlisle–Silloth train at Kirkandrews on 9 April 1955.
Below: Remains of Solway viaduct at Bowness on Solway, 2 April 1975. The
embankment on the north side can be seen across the water near Annan. (*W. A.
Camwell, John Marshall*)

LANCASTER–GLASSON DOCK
ACT: LNWR (New Railways) 22 July 1878 (182).
OPENED: (*gds*) 2 July 1883; (*pass*) 9 July 1883.
CLOSED: (*pass*) 7 July 1930; (*gds*) 7 September 1964.
REMAINS: Most of the trackbed beside Lune Estuary. Attractive brick overbridge near Ashton Hall, 456570. Girder bridge over Conder Estuary, 456560.
USES: Trackbed made into a 5^1/$_2$ mile walk. Area designated 'Site of Special Scientific Interest'. It supports the largest wintering and passage population of wading birds in Britain.

CHAPTER 7: CUMBRIA, SOUTH

FURNESS RAILWAY: ARNSIDE–HINCASTER
ACT: FR, 20 June 1867 (104).
OPENED: 26 June 1876. Heversham station, 1890.
CLOSURES: (*pass*) 4 May 1942; Sandside–Hincaster (*all traffic*) 9 September 1963; Sandside goods station, 17 June 1968; Arnside–Sandside (*all traffic*) 1 January 1972.
REMAINS: almost the entire trackbed is walkable, through pleasant scenery and a rock cutting at Sandside. Beela viaduct has been removed involving a short detour by the road bridge, 488814. Cutting partly filled by viaduct material. Heversham station platform, 497826. Another cutting filled at 512837.
USES: An ugly block of flats occupies Sandside station site.

CONISHEAD PRIORY BRANCH
ACT: FR, 27 June 1876.
OPENED: 27 June 1883.
CLOSED: Conishead Priory station, 1 January 1917.
REMAINS: Trackbed walkable, but in private woodland. Beyond Conishead Priory station, 307756, the formation continues to 307752, but evidently never carried track.
USES: Conishead Priory station now a dwelling.

CONISTON BRANCH
ACTS: Kirkby–Broughton: FR extensions, 27 July 1846 (279); Coniston Railway, 10 August 1857 (110); Furness & Coniston Railways amalgamation, 7 June 1862 (133).
OPENED: Kirkby–Broughton, February 1848; Broughton–Coniston, 18 June 1859.
CLOSED: Broughton first station, 1 June 1859; Foxfield–Coniston

(*pass*) 6 October 1958; (*gds*) 30 April 1962.

REMAINS: Trackbed walkable almost throughout except Foxfield–Broughton where it is closely paralleled by roads. Broughton station and goods shed, 213875. Woodland station, 242904. Goods shed at Torver, 285943.

USES: Broughton, Woodland and Torver stations now private dwellings. Between Park Gate Crossing and Torver a caravan site and access road cover ¼ mile of the trackbed. At Torver ½ mile of the trackbed has been used for improvements to the A593 road. Coniston station site now redeveloped for light industry.

PIEL PIER BRANCH

ACTS: Pile (*sic*) Pier, 27 June 1843 (42); FR, 23 May 1844 (22).

OPENED: Roose Junction–Piel Pier, 24 August 1846; Salthouse Junction–Parrock Junction, 1873; Piel station, Roa Island, October 1881.

CLOSED: Roose Junction–Parrock Hall Junction, and Piel Pier, 1 October 1881; Salthouse Junction–Piel, 6 July 1936.

REMAINS: The embankment to Roa Island is now a road. A few buildings remain on Roa Island, 234648. Some stumps of the pier remain near the shore.

WHITEHAVEN, CLEATOR & EGREMONT RAILWAY

ACTS: Mirehouse Junction–Egremont, and Moor Row–Frizington, 16 June 1854 (64); Frizington–Lamplugh, 7 June 1861 (62); Lamplugh–Marron Junction; north loop at Cleator Moor, 8 June 1863 (64); Egremont–Sellafield: Cleator & Furness Railway, 28 June 1866 (132); Gilgarron branch, Ullock–Distington, 2 August 1875 (191); Distington–Parton, and Mowbray branch, 27 June 1876 (58); vesting in LNWR: LNWR (WC&ER vesting) 28 June 1877 (47); vesting in FR/LNWR: LNWR & FR (WC&ER vesting) 17 June 1878 (95).

OPENED: Mirehouse Junction–Egremont; Moor Row–Frizington (*gds*) 11 January 1857; (*pass*) 1 July 1857; Frizington–Lamplugh (*gds*) November 1862; Frizington–Rowrah (*pass*) 12 February 1864; Lamplugh–Marron Junction (*gds*); Rowrah–Marron Junction (*pass*); Moor Row–Cleator Moor–Birksbridge Junction, April 1866; Egremont–Sellafield, 1 August 1869; deviation at Yeathouse, June 1874; Gilgarron branch, Ullock–Distington, 23 October 1879; Distington–Parton (*gds*) 1879 (*pass*) 1 June 1881.

CLOSURES: Eskett (*pass*) June 1874; (*gds*) 6 February 1931. Distington–Parton (*pass*) 8 December 1883 (re-opened 1 October 1913–1 September 1914); Ullock Junction–Wythemoor colliery, 1919; –Distington and Lowca Junction, 1922; Moor Row–Marron Junction (*pass*) 13 April 1931; Distington–Bain's Siding on Parton branch (*gds*) May 1932; Mirehouse Junction–Egremont–Sellafield (*pass*) 7 January 1935 (re-opened 6 May 1946–16 June 1947); Rowrah–Marron Junction (*gds*) 3 May 1954; Crossfield (*gds*) September 1949; Yeathouse–Rowrah (*gds*) 21 August 1967; Cleator Moor–Yeathouse (*gds*) 4 November 1963; Egremont–Sellafield (*gds*) 2 March 1964; Mirehouse Junction–Cleator Moor and Egremont (*regular freight*) 5 June 1972; Parton–Bain's Siding (probably) May 1973; last train Moor Row–Rowrah Quarry, February 1978. Mirehouse Junction–Moor Row–Egremont–Beckermet Iron Mine (*all traffic*) 6 October 1980.

REMAINS: Sellafield–Moor Row–Mirehouse Junction: Beckermet station, 015065; station house and goods shed. Site of junction with Beckermet mine branch, 010084. Egremont station, 010112; platform, station offices and goods shed. Woodend station, 010129; level-crossing, goods shed, platform and station house. Bigrigg branch junction, 008138; branch dismantled and much overgrown. Moor Row station, 005145; platforms only.

Moor Row–Marron Junction: 1866 loop through Cleator Moor partly built over. Frizington station, 034154; station house, platforms, buildings in goods yard. Site of Mowbray branch junction, 041157. Branch much overgrown. Junctions of original 1857 line at 045161 and 044170; original track and branch to Eskett mine walkable. Yeathouse station, 045166; platforms; coal drops at junction of original line, 044170. Winder station, 048180; house and platform. Rowrah station, 060186; house, platforms and signalbox. Lamplugh station, 066217 (Wright Green until 4 August 1901); station house. Site of Ullock Junction, 071243. Underbridges removed on abandoned section. Little of it is worth the effort of walking.

Ullock Junction–Distington–Parton: Underbridges removed, but track walkable from Ullock to Wythemoor Head. Several stone overbridges. Iron overbridge at 048242 and remains of iron underbridges at 028240 by Fletcher Jennings, Whitehaven. Abutments of bridge over C&WJ at 014232. Track walkable to junction at Distington, 012239. Site of junction at 009241. Site of Lowca branch junction, 994217. (Track to Lowca good for walking or cycling.) Iron bridge over river, 984212. Stub of line remains at Parton Junction, 980209.

USES: Beckermet station house now a dwelling. Goods shed now a garage. Cleator Moor station, 012155, now a housing estate. Goods station on 1857 line, 017153, still used as coal yard. Station houses at Frizington, Winder, Rowrah, Lamplugh now privately occupied. Rowrah station yard still a coal depot. Distington station yard now a stone-crushing plant. Mirehouse Junction–Rowrah: trackbed being converted (1990) into the Whitehaven and Rowrah Railway Path, an 8-mile cycle route.

CLEATOR & WORKINGTON JUNCTION RAILWAY

ACTS: Cleator Moor–Siddick; branch at Workington; Harrington–Rose Hill, 27 June 1876 (51); working by Furness Railway, 28 June 1877 (48); Distington–Rowrah, 4 July 1878 (129); Calva Junction–Linefoot; Cloffocks Junction to Workington Bridge on Cockermouth & Workington line; branch to Harrington harbour; branch to Derwent Ironworks, 16 July 1883 (118); amended by Act of 25 June 1886 (79).

OPENED: Cleator Moor–Workington; Harrington–Rose Hill Junction (*gds*) 1 October 1879; Cleator Moor–Workington Central (*pass*) 1 October 1879; Workington Central–Siddick (*pass*) 1 September 1880; Distington–Rowrah (*gds*) 1 May 1882; Distington–Oatlands (*pass*) September 1888; Oatlands–Arlecdon (*pass*) October 1912; Cloffocks Junction–Workington Bridge, 16 March 1885; branches to Harrington harbour and Derwent Ironworks, 1885; Calva Junction–Linefoot (*gds*) 24 March 1887; Calva Junction–Seaton (*pass*) 4 January 1888; Seaton–Linefoot (*pass*) 1 September 1908; Harrington–Rose Hill (*gds*) *circa* 1877; Harrington–Lowca (*pass*) 2 June 1913.

CLOSURES: Oatlands–Arlecdon (*pass*) 1 January 1917; Distington–Oatlands (*pass*) 1st closure July 1892; re-opened November 1909; 2nd closure 1 January 1917; re-opened July 1917; final closure September 1922; Distington–Rowrah (*gds*) 8 August 1938; Seaton–Linefoot (*pass*) November 1908; Calva Junction–Seaton (*pass*) 1st closure July 1897; re-opened February 1907; final closure February 1922; Buckhill Colliery–Linefoot (*gds*) 1935; Calva Junction–Buckhill Colliery, 1939; Seaton (*gds*) 6 April 1964; Harrington–Rose Hill–Lowca (*pass*) 31 May 1926; Cleator Moor–Siddick (*pass*) 13 April 1931; Cleator Moor–Distington (*gds*) 1 July 1963; Distington– Calva Junction and Derwent branch to Wilkinson's Siding, 15 June

1964; Harrington Junction–Bain's Tramway Junction (Rose Hill) and harbour (Moss Bay) probably May 1973.

REMAINS: Cleator Moor–Siddick: Trackbed much overgrown and in private ownership as far as Distington. Iron underbridges removed. Many stone-arched overbridges remain. Cutting filled-in at site of C&WJ station at Cleator Moor. Arched underbridge and Keekle viaduct, 005164. Moresby Parks station house and gradient post, 997195. From Distington to Workington the trackbed is excellent for both walking and cycling. Junction with Parton line, 010241. High Harrington station platforms, 000255. Junction with Rose Hill branch, 002260 (see Harrington & Lowca Light Railway). Junction with Harrington Harbour branch, 001265. Trackbed suitable for walking and cycling to abutments of bridge over Whitehaven Junction main line, 988265, and down to Harrington Harbour. Stone-arched bridge over B5296 in Workington, 003283. Bridges under main roads in Workington, 004286. Abutments of bridges carrying main line and connection to Workington Bridge over Derwent at Cloffocks, 005291. Rails still in place from Calva Junction to Siddick Junction.

Calva Junction–Linefoot: Rails were still in place from Calva Junction to naval base at site of Buckhill colliery in 1991, used about twice weekly. Seaton station, 018307: two platforms and building on down side. Beyond naval base from road at 067320 trackbed much overgrown. At 076330 it is covered by vast quarry waste tips. Site of Linefoot Junction can be seen beside new road at 079335.

Distington–Rowrah: Site of flyover junction at Distington can be visited from road at 013237. Whole route much overgrown and in private ownership. Several stone-arch overbridges. Oatlands cutting and tunnel, 024220, filled-in. Track can be viewed from road at 027205. Embankment at Brownrigg Curve removed in middle; 046200. Arlecdon station house, 050186.

USES: Station houses at Moresby Parks and Arlecdon occupied as dwellings. Site of Workington Central station, 004286, now a car park, market place and housing estate. From here to road bridge at 005293 the track is in use as a footway over the Derwent on new concrete spans on the old piers.

ROWRAH & KELTON FELL MINERAL RAILWAY
ACT: 16 July 1874 (146).
OPENED: January 1877.

CLOSED: 1933.

REMAINS: Almost whole route walkable, but not easy; most underbridges removed. Fine scenery at upper end.

HARRINGTON & LOWCA LIGHT RAILWAY
Light Railway Order confirmed 16 May 1913.
OPENED: (pass) 2 June 1913.
CLOSED: (pass) 31 May 1926; *(gds)* May 1973 (?).
REMAINS: From Harrington Junction, 002260, trackbed is good for walking or cycling to Lowca, with fine views over the sea. Rose Hill station, 993250; platform. Site of Rose Hill Junction, 990249. Trackbed walkable down to Harrington Harbour but bridge removed over Whitehaven Junction line. Copperas Hill station, 988245; platform and brick building. Lowca station, 979218; some brick walling. Ground subsided.

CHAPTER 8: CUMBRIA, NORTH

COCKERMOUTH & WORKINGTON RAILWAY
ACTS: C&WR, 21 July 1845 (120); absorption by LNWR, 16 July 1866 (189).
OPENED: 28 April 1847.
CLOSED: Cockermouth C&W station *(pass)* 2 January 1865; Marron Junction *(pass)* 1 July 1897; Broughton Cross, 2 March 1942; Workington Bridge, 1 January 1951; Camerton, 3 March 1952; Workington–Cockermouth (–Keswick) *(gds)* 1 June 1964; *(pass)* 18 April 1966.
REMAINS: Abutments of bridges over Derwent at 024296, 030300, 039306, 046305, 049303. Short sections of trackbed between are difficult of access and scarcely worth walking. Site of Marron East and West Junctions, 057301, accessible down track from Nepgill, 060294, above Bridgefoot. Through plate-girder span over Marron and about a mile of trackbed suitable for walking. Broughton Cross station house, 076304. Stone viaduct, twelve spans, 222ft (67.7m) long beside road and bridge over A595, 114306.
USES: At Workington, 000295–001294 trackbed landscaped and now a pleasant riverside walk. From 065300, ½ mile (1km) east of Marron Junction to 105309 west of Cockermouth trackbed absorbed by A66(T) road. Broughton Cross station house occupied.

COCKERMOUTH, KESWICK & PENRITH

ACTS: (Cockermouth & Workington Extension Railway, 3 August 1846 (343); line not built); CK&P Act, 1 August 1861 (203); Redhills Curve: NER (Auckland and other branches) 23 June 1864 (67).

OPENED: Cockermouth–Keswick (*gds*) 1 November 1864; Cockermouth–Penrith all traffic, 2 January 1865; Redhills Curve, NER, 5 September 1866.

CLOSED: Blencow (*pass*) 3 March 1952; re-opened 2 July 1956. (Workington)–Cockermouth–Keswick (*pass*) 18 April 1966. Keswick–Penrith (*pass*) 6 March 1972. Flusco Quarry–Penrith (*gds*) 19 June 1972.

REMAINS: Trackbed from Cockermouth to A66(T) at 145298. Embleton station house, 164302. Bassenthwaite Lake station house, 119310. Braithwaite station house, 235242. Trackbed walkable from where A66(T) turns-off at 232246 west of Keswick to A594 bridge at 279238, and from Briery Mill platform, 285241, through Greta valley to 315246 west of Threlkeld. This is a fine walk. Keswick station, 270238: handsome slate building with three gables; down platform and awning. Bowstring deck span over Greta and plate-girder bridge over A594, 274237. Tunnel blocked by new road embankment. Platform at Briery Mill. Two bowstring deck spans over Greta, 287243; another at 288244; bowstring through spans over Greta, 294246 and 299246; bowstring deck span over Greta, 305245; horseshoe-arched brick-lined tunnel 21yd (19m) and bowstring through skew span over Greta, 306245; rock cutting; bowstring through span over Greta 314248. All these bridges are strengthened with plate girders beneath. Iron plate-girder span of 75ft (23m) over Greta, 316246. Threlkeld station, 320245: island platform with buildings and signal box all in ruined state. Iron lattice footbridge over cutting. Mosedale viaduct, 355258, twelve arches of 30ft (9.1m) 404ft (123m) long over Mosedale Beck. Troutbeck station, 390270: station building, signal box and stone shed remain. The stone road overbridge was demolished in 1984. The road now crosses the trackbed on the level. Trackbed walkable to Penruddock station, 435280, but underbridges and embankment removed at road junctions at 428278. Penruddock station, 435280: staggered platforms; buildings derelict. Stone viaduct of five arches about 40ft (12m) high, 429280. Rock cutting with retaining walls, 434279. From Flusco quarry, 456290, to Blencow, 464304, track walkable, with fine views. Blencow station: station building and platforms. Sections of track walkable to Penrith.

USES: Cockermouth station site now headquarters of Cumbria Fire Service, built 1985. From 145298 near Cockermouth along the west shore of Bassenthwaite Lake to 232246 near Keswick the trackbed is covered by the new A66(T) road. Embleton station house now private dwelling. Keswick station now houses model shop and a model railway. Keswick–Threlkeld: trackbed converted into the Keswick Railway Footpath, a 4-mile walk, in use by 1986. May be extended to Troutbeck. Troutbeck station building now a dwelling. Blencow station buildings enlarged as dwelling; goods yard now occupied by garage and lorry depot.

MARYPORT & CARLISLE RAILWAY
Mealsgate Loop
ACT: M&C, 30 June 1862 (80).
OPENED: Aspatria–Mealsgate (*gds*) 2 April 1866; (*pass*) 26 November 1866; Mealsgate–Aikbank Junction, 1 October 1878.
CLOSED: Aikbank Junction–Mealsgate, 1 August 1921; Aspatria–Mealsgate (*pass*) 22 September 1930; (*gds*) 1 December 1952.
REMAINS: Track much overgrown and all iron underbridges removed. Several stone overbridges. Blennerhasset station, 179419; part of platform. Mealsgate station house, 207425.
USES: At Blennerhasset bungalows have been built on the station site. Mealsgate station house now a dwelling.
Bullgill–Brigham branch
ACT: M&C, 19 June 1865 (84).
OPENED: (*gds*) 12 April 1867; (*pass*) 1 June 1867.
CLOSED: Linefoot station (*pass*) November 1908; (*gds*) 1 September 1921; whole line, 29 April 1935.
REMAINS: Much of track overgrown and underbridges removed; some sections cleared and returned to agricultural use. Short stretches are walkable. Several stone overbridges. Dovenby Lodge station, 095326: two-storey house and platform. Papcastle station, 091315: large station house. Abutments of bridge over Derwent, 089311.
USES: Station houses at Dovenby Lodge and Papcastle now dwellings. Cutting at 094325 used as refuse tip.

CARLISLE–PORT CARLISLE AND SILLOTH
ACTS: Carlisle Canal, 6 April 1819 (13); Port Carlisle Dock & Railway, 4 August 1853 (119); Carlisle & Silloth Bay Railway & Dock,

16 July 1855 (153); lease of undertakings to NBR, 3 June 1862 (47) and (48); amalgamation with NBR, 12 August 1880 (167).

OPENED: Carlisle–Port Carlisle: canal 1823; railway (*gds*) 22 May 1854; (*pass*) 22 June 1854; Drumburgh Junction–Silloth (*pass*) 22 June 1856; (*gds*) (probably) 26 August 1856.

CLOSED: Drumburgh Junction–Port Carlisle, 1 June 1932; Carlisle–Silloth (*gds*) 1 June 1964; (*pass*) 7 September 1964.

REMAINS: Much of the route from Carlisle to Drumburgh and Port Carlisle looks so like a derelict canal that anyone might be forgiven for believing that it had been abandoned for a century and that there was never a railway along its bed. Parts are overgrown or flooded. Many of the iron overbridges, shored up underneath, have rounded sandstone abutments as if built for a canal. Kirkandrews station, 352585. Beyond here the formation has been obliterated. Stations at Burgh by Sands and Drumburgh cleared without trace. At Port Carlisle is the remains of a platform, 241623. Abbey Town station house, 173507; Silloth station, 109533: buildings survive in modified condition; sidings area now playing fields.

USES: Station houses at Kirkandrews and Abbey Town now dwellings.

SOLWAY JUNCTION RAILWAY

ACTS: Kirtlebridge to the M&C at Brayton, 30 June 1864 (158); deviations, 29 June 1865 (186); junction with Silloth line, 15 July 1867 (116); purchase of Annan–Kirtlebridge section, CR, 5 August 1873 (228); branch to join Port Carlisle branch (not built) 10 August 1882 (188); transfer to CR: CR, 6 July 1895 (132).

OPENED: 8 August 1870.

CLOSED: 1 January 1917; re-opened 2 March 1919; final closure (*pass*) 20 May 1921; (*gds*) 1 September 1921; Abbey Town–Brayton re-opened (*gds*) May 1922; closed 13 February 1933. Solway viaduct demolished 1934–5.

REMAINS: Embankment into Solway and several piers of viaduct, 212628. Bowness station, 214623. Most of the trackbed now returned to agricultural use and obliterated.

USES: Bowness station house now a dwelling.

Acknowledgements

In the preparation of the first edition my principal thanks were to Professor Allan Patmore, editor of this series, whose interest and practical suggestions were most encouraging. Field work involved hundreds of miles of travelling on foot, bicycle and by train and car to inspect all the abandoned railways; and numerous local people answered my queries. Much useful help was received from the staffs of Barrow in Furness Library, the County Record Offices of Lancashire at Preston and of Cumbria at Carlisle. Others to whom I am grateful for information are Messrs H.D. Bowtell, Allan Brackenbury, John Ryan and F.D. Smith. Mr W.A. Camwell kindly supplied a large number of photographs from which several were selected.

In preparation of this new edition I have received tremendous help from Roger W. Howarth of Bolton who, with meticulous attention to detail, has made corrections and has noted many changes which have taken place in the last decade. He has also made numerous useful additions to the Gazetteer and Bibliography.

Bibliography

Abbreviations used:

BLS	Branch Line Society
BT	*Back Track*
CRA	Cumbrian Railways Association
D & C	David & Charles PLC, Publishers
HMSO	Her Majesty's Stationery Office
L & YRS	Lancashire & Yorkshire Railway Society
LRSS	Liverpool Road Station Society
MRIAS	Manchester Region Industrial Archaeological Society
MTMS	Manchester Transport Museum Society
R & CHS	Railway & Canal Historical Society
RM	Railway Magazine
RO	*The Railway Observer* (Journal of the Railway Correspondence & Travel Society)
RW	*Railway World*
TI	*Trains Illustrated*

GENERAL

Appleton, J.H.: *Disused railways in the countryside of England and Wales* , HMSO, 1970

Biddle, Gordon: *Railway stations in the North West,* Dalesman, 1981

Bradshaw: *Railway Guides*

Bradshaw: *Railway Manuals,* 1849–1923

Clinker, C.R.: *Register of closed passenger stations and goods depots 1830-1977* , Avon Anglia, 1978

Daniels, Gerald & Dench, Les: *Passengers no more,* Ian Allan, 1980

Elis, Rhys ab: *Railway rights of way,* BLS, 1985

Gammell, C.J.: *LMS Branch lines, 1945–1965,* Oxford Publishing Company, 1980

Gilbert, A.C. & Knight, N.R.: *Railways around Lancashire: a pictorial survey,* MTMS, 1975

Greville, M.D.: *Chronological list of the railways of Cheshire 1837-1939,* R & CHS, 1973

Greville,M.D.: *Chronological list of the railways of Lancashire 1828–1939,* R & CHS, 1973

Grimshaw, John and Associates: *Study of disused railways in England and Wales,* HMSO, 1982

Holt, G.O.: *A regional history of the railways of Great Britain Vol 10 The North West,* D & C, 1978

Joy, David: *Railways in Lancashire,* Dalesman, 1975

Joy, David: *Railways in the North: a pictorial introduction,* Dalesman, 1983

Lewthwaite, G.C.: *Branch Line Index,* BLS, 1971

Marshall, John: *The Lancashire & Yorkshire Railway* Vols 1 and 2, D & C, 1969, 1970

Railway Clearing House: *Handbook of stations,* RCH,1938

Railway Clearing House: *Railway junction diagrams 1915,* D & C, 1969
Shannon, Paul & Hillmer, John: *British Railways past and present* No 3 *The North West,* Silver Link Publishing, 1986
Somerville, Christopher: *Walking old railways,* D & C, 1979
Thomas, David St John: *The rural transport problem,* Routledge & Kegan Paul, 1963
Vinter, Jeff: *Railway walks: LMS,* Alan Sutton, 1990
Whishaw, Francis: *Railways of Great Britain & Ireland 1843,* D & C, 1969
Wignall, C.J.: *Complete British Railways maps and gazetteer,* Oxford Publishing Co, 1983

CHAPTER1 : IN AND AROUND MANCHESTER
Bardsley, J.R.: *The railways of Bolton 1824—1959,* New edition, Author, 1981
Bolger, Paul: *An illustrated history of the Cheshire Lines Committee,* Heyday, n.d.
Bowtell, Harold D.: *Reservoir railways of Manchester and the Peak,* Oakwood Press, 1977
Christiansen, Rex & Miller, R.W.: *The North Staffordshire Railway,* D & C, 1971
Dow, George : *Great Central* Vol 2, Ian Allan, 1962
Dyckhoff, Nigel: *The Cheshire Lines Committee then and now,* Ian Allan, 1984
Fields, N., Gilbert, A.C. & Knight, N.R.: *Liverpool to Manchester: into the second century,* MTMS, 1980
Fox, Gregory K.: *The railways around Stockport,* Foxline Publishing, 1986
Fox, Peter.: 'Light rail revolution', RM, January 1990
Gilbert, A.C. & Knight, N.R.: *Railways around Manchester: a pictorial review of the nineteen-fifties,* MTMS, 1973
Greville, M. D. & Holt, G. O.: 'Railway development in Manchester', RM, September, October, November 1957
Griffiths, R. P.: *The Cheshire Lines Railway,* Oakwood Press, 1958
Jeuda, Basil.: *Railways of the Macclesfield district,* Wyvern, 1985
Johnson, E.M.: *Manchester railway termini,* Foxline Publishing, 1987
Johnson, E.M.: *Railways in and around the Manchester suburbs: a selective pictorial review,* Foxline Publishing, 1989
Makepeace, Chris (editor): *Oldest in the world: the story of Liverpool Road station, Manchester, 1830–1980,* LRSS/MRIAS, 1980
Marshall, John: 'The first railway in Lancashire.' RM, August 1978
Rose, R.E.: *The LMS and LNER in Manchester,* Ian Allan, 1987
Simpson, Bill: *Railways in and around Bolton: an historical review,* Foxline Publishing, 1990
Singleton, David: *Liverpool & Manchester Railway,* Dalesman, 1975
— 'New goods station, Great Northern Railway, Manchester', *The Engineer,* Vol 86, 2 September 1898, pp223–5

CHAPTER 2 : EAST LANCASHIRE
Bairstow, Martin: *The Leeds, Huddersfield & Manchester Railway,* Author, 1984. Revised edition, 1990
Bairstow, Martin: *The Manchester & Leeds Railway,* Author, 1987
Bairstow, Martin: *Railways in East Lancashire,* Author, 1988
Fox, Michael & Fox, Peter: 'The Delph branch', BT, Vol 3 No 2, April/June 1989
Fox, Michael & Fox, Peter: *The Delph Donkey: a local railway,* Authors, 1984
Fraser, N.: 'The Delph branch', RW, March 1963
Fraser, N.: 'Oldham, Ashton-under-Lyne & Guide Bridge Junction Railway',

RO, June 1963.

Greenwood, H.: 'The end of the Werneth Incline', RW, February 1963

Kardas, Handel: 'East Lancs advances', RW, May 1990

Roberts, B.: *Railways and mineral tramways of Rossendale*, Oakwood Press, 1974

Rush, R.W.: *The East Lancashire Railway*, Oakwood Press, 1983

Seville, H.: 'Oldham and its railways', RM, April 1927

Wells, Jeffrey: 'The Werneth Incline', BT, Vol 4 No 1, January/February 1990

Westall, David: *The Holcombe Brook branch*, L & Y RS, 1988

Wilby, C. Richard: *Railways around East Lancashire*, Wyvern, 1983

Wray, Tom: *The Bacup branch: Ramsbottom–Stubbins– Rawtenstall*, L & Y RS, 1985

Wray, Tom: *The Bacup branch: Rochdale–Facit–Bacup*, L & YRS, 1989

CHAPTER 3 : MERSEYSIDE

Box, C.E.: *The Liverpool Overhead Railway.*, Railway World Ltd, 1959

Christiansen, Rex: 'Forgotten railways of the Wirral', RM, June 1990

Clark, Rhodri: 'Mendelssohn. The Liverpool & Manchester's first passenger', *British Railway Journal* No 35 Winter 1991

Gahan, John W.: *Seventeen stations to Dingle: The Liverpool Overhead Railway remembered*, Countyvise, 1982

Greville, M.D. & Holt, G.O. : 'Railway development in Liverpool', RM, February, March, April 1959.

Highet, C.: *The Wirral Railway.*, Oakwood Press, 1961

Mendelssohn, Felix: *Felix Mendelssohn: a life in letters*, Ed by Rudolf Elvers. Translated from German by Craig Tomlinson. Cassell, 1986

Mercer, B.: 'The LNWR and Liverpool', RM, September 1914

Merseyside Railway History Group: *The Hooton to West Kirby branch line and the Wirral Way*, Metropolitan Borough of Wirral, 1982

Shannon, Paul & Hillmer, John: *British Railways past and present* No 6 *Cheshire and North Wales*, Silver Link Publishing, 1988

CHAPTER 4 : WEST LANCASHIRE

Biddle, Gordon: *The railways around Preston: an historical review*, Foxline Publishing, 1989

Cotterall, J.E.: *The West Lancashire Railway*, Oakwood Press, 1982

Gairns, J.F.: 'West Coast Lines of the LNER', RM, October 1924. (Includes Silloth and Port Carlisle lines and Southport & Cheshire Lines Extension)

Parker, Norman: *The Preston & Longridge Railway*, Oakwood Press, 1972

Perkins, T.R.: 'Garstang & Knot End Railway' (sic), RM, January 1908.

Rush, R.W. & Price, M.R.: *The Garstang & Knott End Railway.*, New edition, Oakwood Press, 1985

Sekon, G.A.: 'The Knott End Railway', RM, December 1924

CHAPTER 5 : BETWEEN BACKBURN AND ST HELENS

Dow, George: *Great Central* Vols 2 and 3, Ian Allan 1962, 1965.

Marshall, John: 'The Lancashire Union Railways', RM, April, May, June 1970

CHAPTER 6 : THE LUNE VALLEY

Anderson, V.R. & Fox, G.K.: 'Station studies: Lancaster (Green Ayre)', BT, Vol 1 No 3, Autumn 1987

Binns, Donald: *The 'Little' North Western Railway*, Wyvern, 1982

Jenkins, Stanley C.: 'The Glasson Dock branch', *British Railway Journal* No 16, Spring 1987

Hamilton, J.A.B.: 'The Ingleton Branch of the LMS', RM, September 1934

Machell, G.: 'The Clapham–Ingleton–Low Gill line', RW, December 1954
Nuttall, K. & Rawlings, T.: *Railways around Lancaster*, Dalesman, 1980
Pearsall, A.W.H.: 'The Ingleton branch' ,RM, June 1954
Western, Robert: *The Ingleton branch: a lost route to Scotland*, Oakwood Press, 1990 (First published in 1971 as *The Lowgill branch*)

CHAPTERS 7 AND 8 : CUMBRIA
Allen, Cecil J. (*Voyageur*): 'The Cockermouth, Keswick, & Penrith Railway', RM, August 1921; and TI, October 1961
Allen, Cecil J.: 'Maryport & Carlisle Railway', RM, October 1909
Andrews, M.: 'The origins of the Furness Railway', R & CHS *Journal*, October 1965, January 1966
Barbey, M.F.: 'From Carlisle to Silloth', RM, February 1955
Bowtell, Harold D.: *Rails through Lakeland – an illustrated history of the Workington–Cockermouth–Keswick–Penrith Railway 1847–1972*, Silver Link Publishing Ltd, 1989
Broughton, John & Harris, Nigel: *British Railways past and present* No 1 *Cumbria*, Silver Link Publishing, 1985
Cumbrian Railways Association: *The Coniston Railway*, CRA, 1985
Davey, C.R.: *Reflections of the Furness Railway*, Lakeland Heritage Books, 1984
Earnshaw, Alan: 'The Port Carlisle branch', BT, Vol 3 No 3 July/August 1989
Earnshaw, Alan: 'The Silloth branch' Part 1, BT, Vol 4 No 4, July/August 1990; Part 2, Vol 4 No 5, September/October 1990
Edgar, Stuart & Sinton, John M.: *The Solway Junction Railway*, Oakwood Press, 1990
Gradon, W. McGowan: *Furness Railway, its rise and development 1846–1923*, Author, 1946
Gradon, W.M.: *A history of the Cockermouth, Keswick & Penrith Railway.*, Author, 1948
Gradon, W.M.: *The track of the ironmasters*. A history of the Cleator & Workington Junction Railway, Author, 1952
Gradon, W.M.: 'The Rowrah & Kelton Fell Mineral Railway', RM, March 1952
Joy, David: *Cumbrian Coast railways*, Dalesman, 1968
Joy, David: *Railways of the Lake Counties*, Dalesman, 1973
Joy, David: *A regional history of the railways of Great Britain* Vol 14 *The Lake Counties*, D&C, 1983
Melville, J. & Hobbs, J.L.: *Early railway history in Furness*, Cumberland & Westmorland Antiquarian & Archaeological Society, 1951
Mullay, A.J.: 'Annan and the Solway Viaduct', BT, Vol 2 No 2, Summer 1988
Robinson, Peter W.: *Railways of Cumbria*, Dalesman, 1980
Rush, R.W.: *The Furness Railway*, Oakwood Press, 1973
Sankey, Raymond & Norman, K.J.: *The Furness Railway: a photographic recollection*, Dalesman, 1977
Simmons, Jack: *The Maryport & Carlisle Railway*, Oakwood Press, 1947
Thomas, David St John: *Lake District Transport Report*, D&C, 1961
Webb, D.R.: 'Between the Solway and Sellafield', RM, September, October 1964
White, Stephen: *Lakeland steam: a celebration of the Cockermouth, Keswick & Penrith Railway, 1861–1972*, Carel Press, 1985
White, Stephen: *Solway steam: the story of the Silloth and Port Carlisle railways 1854–1964*, Carel Press, 1984

—: 'The Cleator & Workington Junction Railway', RM, September 1912

Index